THE LITTLE
BLACK BOOK OF
BUSINESS
REPORTS

THE LITTLE
BLACK BOOK OF
BUSINESS
REPORTS

MICHAEL C. THOMSETT

American Management Association

This book is available at a special
discount when ordered in bulk quantities.
For information, contact Special Sales Department,
AMACOM, a division of American Management Association,
135 West 50th Street, New York, NY 10020.

LIBRARY OF CONGRESS
Library of Congress Cataloging-in-Publication Data

Thomsett, Michael C.
    The little black book of business reports / Michael C. Thomsett.
      p. cm.
    Includes index.
    ISBN 0-8144-7693-7
    1. Business report writing. I. Title.
HF5719.T46   1988   88-47712
808'.066651—dc19   CIP

Printing number

10 9 8 7 6 5 4 3 2

For Dino

Contents

Introduction

"The only thing that saves us from the bureaucracy is its inefficiency."

—Eugene McCarthy

The new employee wrote her first report during her second month on the job. She waited a week, then anxiously asked her boss for a response. "To the report?" the surprised manager asked. "No one actually reads those things. It's enough that it was completed on time."

That's the problem with reports in some companies. Everyone thinks it's extremely important that reports be written, but they are never put to any use afterwards. And there are reasons for this.

Sometimes the format of the report obscures the message, because the format is too complex. The format may have been developed over time from a hybrid of requirements, so that the final report is too cryptic or disorganized; or the format may have been designed by someone who did not understand the report's purpose.

One more element that every report should have—one that most reports lack—is a conclusion and recommendation section. A report should not just summarize the past or present status of a department, budget, or project; it should do much more. It is assumed that the person responsible for preparing a report is an expert in the subject area and that person should take charge of the report and tell management what

1

actions should be taken now—whether to reverse a negative situation, reinforce a positive one, or achieve a goal in the future. Doing that will make your reports indispensable. Reports are useful tools for management, but only if they are conceived and prepared properly.

If you have never prepared a report but expect that you will be asked to prepare one in the near future, it's natural to fear the process. But a report is nothing more than a collection of information, prepared in a particular format. An *effective* report is prepared with a purpose and a reader in mind. It directs the reader's attention to the most important information at once and supports that with evidence in various forms.

This book shows you how to design and write reports that will be read and used, that will help others do their jobs better, and that will help you become an effective and valued source for information. It explains the many uses of this basic business communications device. You will find the different standard formats as well as guidance on selecting the best one for your own reports. You will learn how to design reports that combine flowcharts with narrative explanations, incorporate simple graphs and charts, and arrange information so that the reader's job is enjoyable and easy.

You communicate orally on the job all the time. A written report should be nothing more than an effective summary of knowledge you have or knowledge you can discover within your own area of expertise. And when you think of a report that way, problems are more easily solved and overcome.

Consider this little black book as a type of report itself, a collection of personal trade secrets for your own use. It presents solutions through examples and work projects. It shows you how to inform others using simple but practical techniques. A good report—like a good book—is not necessarily thick or complex. So treat this little black book as you would any confidential internal report. Keep it from curious eyes, preferably under lock and key. Like all valuable information, your personal trade secrets should be protected with great care.

1

The Purpose of Reports

"I never let my schooling interfere with my education."

—Mark Twain

One manager told another, "I asked for a report from one of the employees in my department, and he finished it in less than one day. It makes me nervous." The other asked why, and the first one answered, "He rushed off to get started so quickly that I didn't get a chance to tell him the subject of the report."

With so much emphasis on the proper way to do a report, some of us never get around to asking *why* it's being written. If you understand that the purpose should be the starting point of report preparation, the "how-to" is obvious. If you always begin with the purpose, you are already writing more effective and successful reports.

A good report conveys information, interprets it, and provides value. It is designed for a specific audience, e.g., the board of directors, your supervisor, or someone outside the company. But no matter who the reader is, you should always ask:

1. Who will read this report?
2. Why is the report needed?
3. What is needed in order to make a decision?

These three focal points—the reader, the reason, and the content—define every report. Without them, your reports cannot be valid, because you haven't yet defined your purpose. But with these points, you are ready to take the next step—addressing the specific request.

REQUEST AND RESPONSE

If you remember the focal points whenever you prepare a report, your focus will always be strong. You will be able to concentrate on essentials and eliminate what you don't need.

It isn't enough to provide basic information and expect the reader to interpret it. By drawing conclusions, your reports point the way to solutions, something that most reports lack. They don't go beyond the collection of raw data and thus do not show the reader how to proceed. Once you have a focus on the purpose of the report, you will be able to show others how to solve problems. Give answers, not just information.

The recipient of the typical report is frustrated time and again. A request is made, and a report is produced. It lists information related to the issue, but does not really solve the problem. For example:

Request: Prepare a report that lists the current status of projects compared to deadline and explains why some are behind schedule.

Response: The report lists each project and completion status, and shows whether it is on schedule or behind.

Problem: The response lists the components of a problem, but does not explain *why* or *how* the problem developed. It also fails to offer solutions.

Request: Compile an analysis of budgeting procedures and their effectiveness.

Response: The report describes how budgets are prepared, who does the work, and what forms of follow-up are used each month.

Problem: The report does not address the central issue: Is the current procedure the best possible way to control budgets? By simply listing the way budgets are done now, the report does not tell the reader anything new. To be useful, it should also identify weaknesses and offer solutions.

Reports that fail to respond properly are so common that management often accepts them as par for the course. If you speak out, take a stand, and make observations that will improve conditions and procedures, you will be an exceptional employee. Paradoxically, that's why so few people take the trouble, because taking a stand leads to a high profile, which invites criticism. If you are wrong, if your ideas don't work, or if someone disagrees with you, then you make enemies and risk your security in the organization. This defensive thinking is not healthy for your career. If you are willing to offer solutions that save money, improve conditions, and solve problems, you will gain the reputation as a valuable resource. Management needs ideas and promotes creative, progressive people who express them. One of the best forums for expression is in your reports.

PURPOSE AND THE ANALYSIS OF FACTS

The three elements of reader, reason, and content are only the preliminaries in a valuable report. You must also be able to interpret information in a way that enlightens the reader.

Example: The vice president asks you for an analysis of production in a manufacturing plant. He says that there's a problem of falling productivity on the night shift and asks you for a report with ideas for solutions.

You discover that out of three shifts, two show increases in the rate of production for the past six months based on units produced. Only the third shift (midnight to 8 A.M.) shows a decline, so overall the results are positive:

Shift	Rate
1	+13%
2	+ 8%
3	− 6%
Total	+15%

Your first tendency is to give results by shift to show management where the problems are occurring. But after speaking with the vice president of the manufacturing division, you conclude that there's really no problem because, out of a total of 420 workers, one third have been with the company less than six months. New employees start out on the third shift, which is considered a training shift. Upon completion of one month's training, they are rotated to other shifts.

The manufacturing division's vice president explains that putting inexperienced workers in with other shifts would slow down production overall. You realize that the decline in productivity on the night shift is not a negative factor, and your report reads:

> The manufacturing division has increased its overall rate of production by 15% during the last six months. This rate was achieved by isolating training of new employees on one shift.

You were told to prepare a report that explained a perceived problem, but during your investigation, you discover that there's no problem at all. Now you have the opportunity to prepare a valuable report.

Offering "solutions" for what appears to be a negative trend would be misleading. The point isn't that productivity on one shift was lower but that smart scheduling enabled the division to bring about improved productivity overall. Get to the truth underlying the numbers, and be aware that what appears obvious is misleading. Become not just a reporter but an investigator, and consider every detail before you draw and report conclusions.

SAMPLE REPORTS

Reports are classified into several general types: information, study, expert, status, and recommendation. Some reports contain elements of two or more types. Each type of report addresses a specific purpose or range of purposes:

Type	*Purpose*
Information	Conveys and explains facts that the recipient does not have at hand.
Study	Addresses a specified problem and the alternative solutions available, with analysis and recommendations.
Expert	Interprets facts from a particular point of view that requires expertise (the expert who prepares the report might be an outside consultant or a department manager).
Status	Updates the recipient on the current condition of a project, job, venture, or plan.
Recommendation	Proposes something new, such as expanding responsibilities or changing an existing policy or procedure.

The following are samples of each type of report. They show how definition sections can be brief and to the point. We have left out detailed information that would vary greatly in each report you do. Check definition and assignment descriptions to determine how each type of report applies to you.

Information

Definition:	A report that conveys, arranges, or interprets facts.
Assignment:	Prepare a report explaining the rules for entering into contracts with consultants.
Reader:	Vice president.
Reason:	To protect the company when entering a contract with a nonemployee.
Content:	Provisions to be covered and sample contract.

The following is a summary of the provisions that should be included in a contract with an independent consultant.

Sources for information include the corporate attorney and several books from the company's library. The report also includes a recommendation for revisions to our existing consultation contract.

Conclusion: The contract now in use is out of date and should be revised in consultation with legal resources.

Recommendation: Request our corporate attorney to draft an updated consultation contract, along the guidelines presented in this report.

This new contract should be completed and approved before the company enters into any new contracts or renews existing agreements.

Contract provisions: Every consultation contract should contain the following provisions:

1. Definition of independent status, specifying that the consultant is responsible for income taxes and insurance.
2. A statement that the outside consultant may have other clients, sets his or her own working hours, and may work in an outside office or in corporate offices.
3. A statement that the consultant does not report to an in-house supervisor as an employee.
4. Definition section: Each agreed-upon task shall be defined in writing, including the fee, method and timing of payments, specific goals of the project, and a deadline.

Details: [Include photocopies from books or reference to them, a draft of the proposed contract if one has been prepared, and a suggested procedure for hiring consultants and defining scope of projects.]

Study

Definition:	A report that examines a problem and its possible solutions, and then recommends the best course of action.
Assignment:	Propose solutions to the department's backlog of work.
Reader:	Immediate supervisor.
Reason:	To suggest how to manage work flow in excess of ex-

pected levels, and to reduce the incidence of late responses.

Content: Facts of departmental work–flow trends; analysis of possible solutions.

This is an evaluation of what the department must do to correct
the problem of excessive work loads. Since September, outgoing
work has been late and response time inhibited because work
loads are twice as high as in the past.

A study of recent increases in departmental work load indicates the need to hire an additional employee. Company revenues
have grown by 74 percent without a corresponding increase in the
department's size. We are processing nearly twice as many transactions as we did one year ago.

Conclusion: The total salary expenses in the department will
not rise as a result of hiring a new employee. Reducing the
overhead at time-and-a-half that has been occurring over the past
three months will more than offset the additional expense of a new
clerical employee at the assumed hourly rate of pay.

Other alternatives include:

1. *Transferring some responsibilities to other departments.*
   This is not recommended because processes are specialized in our area and no other department is suited to the
   nature of our work.
2. *Making no changes.* The cost of overtime plus the problems created by slow response have created a higher rate
   of errors and affected morale of employees. Accepting this
   condition is not a practical response.
3. *Changing procedures.* Our work processes are not suited
   to automation, and no method for improving significantly on
   efficiency is apparent.

Recommendation: A new clerical employee should be hired
as soon as possible, based upon the attached proposed job
description.

Details: *[Here, a proposed job description is included. Also
include a summary of overhead hours and total expense to the
company, to support your conclusion that hiring an additional
employee will actually cut costs. Show this on a comparative*

chart. Also include a summary of work load now as compared to the past.]

Expert

Definition: A report that interprets information and evaluates condi-
                tions from a particular point of view and suggests solu-
                tions and other actions based on expert knowledge or
                experience.

Assignment: Examine performance of corporate investments in line
                with forecasts, analyze unfavorable variances, and pro-
                pose improvements in procedures.

Reader: President.

Reason: To establish a procedure for management of a corporate
                investment portfolio, within the guidelines of safety de-
                fined by corporate policy.

Content: Analysis of investment performance.

The attached report summarizes investment performance for the first six months of the fiscal year and recommends updating the procedure for managing marketable securities.

Investments are currently managed by an outside broker with no direct management responsibility within the company. However, our agreement with the broker was entered into three years ago when corporate securities were valued at approximately $100,000. Today, we have $1.1 million under management.

Conclusion: We have outgrown the present arrangement and now need to retain an inside investment manager.

Recommendation:

1. Recruit a professional investment manager as a full-time employee whose exclusive responsibilities will be to manage investments along the lines of a corporate investment policy.
2. Draft an investment policy.

Details: *[Include suggested job description for an investment manager and a proposed statement of investment policy. Also include results of your research on salary ranges, and list means for locating a professional manager.]*

Status

Definition:	A report that updates conditions or a situation, anticipates future shortcomings, and recommends solutions that are needed today.
Assignment:	Summarize the status of 14 projects currently in progress for clients, and report on completion status in comparison to schedule deadlines.
Reader:	Immediate supervisor.
Reason:	To update the status of projects and to identify or anticipate scheduling problems, locate causes and correct negative factors, and recommend a course of action.
Content:	Schedule summary comparing actual completion to scheduled completion dates; recommendations for corrective action where needed.

This is a status report of 14 ongoing projects for customers. The purpose of this report is to identify projects that are behind schedule and to recommend corrective actions.

Of the 14 projects, 10 are on or ahead of schedule. No problems are expected in meeting the planned completion dates. Four of the projects are behind schedule.

Conclusion: Three projects have been delayed due to internal workload problems, overly optimistic scheduling, or unanticipated complications in the nature of work. The fourth project is delayed because of revisions requested by the customer.

Recommendation: In the three projects behind schedule for internal reasons, management should consider:

1. Contacting the client and advising that a delay is necessary; or
2. Assigning more staff members to projects to meet the original deadlines.

Also recommended is an evaluation of scheduling procedures to anticipate and correct future deadline problems.

The customer who requested revisions should be advised that because of those changes, the original deadline must be extended.

Details: *[Include a chart that summarizes the schedule and*

completion dates for each of the 14 projects, and include docu-
mentation showing causes of delay.]

Recommendation

Definition: A report that suggests changes in procedures, responsi-
                bility, or policies, or that proposes spending money to
                improve efficiency or profits.
Assignment: No assignment given. This report is generated by you
                and its purpose is to request that the company buy a new
                photocopy machine for your department.
Reader: Immediate supervisor.
Reason: To justify investing in a new photocopying machine.
Content: Analysis of expense history and projection of future
                expense levels and savings.

This is a proposal for an action that will save the company an estimated $3,500 per year.

All supervisors on the third floor endorse the purchase of an additional photocopy machine, on the basis of a study of work load under today's conditions. Included in the analysis is an estimate of lost time due to maintenance problems and excessive demand on a single machine.

Conclusion: The photocopy machine located on the third floor is not designed for the volume of copies being made each month. At the time the machine was purchased, there were 11 employees in three departments on the floor. Today we have 38 employees in five departments.

The machine was designed for a moderate volume of use. We are producing a heavy volume, according to a consultation with the manufacturer. This accounts in part for excessive downtime due to maintenance problems. The machine's age is also responsible for some of the downtime.

These problems lead to loss of time while employees wait in line to use the only copier and delays in completion of assignments due to maintenance problems or backing up of work at the machine.

Recommendation: As the attached worksheets reveal, the cost of inconvenience and delay is conservatively estimated at $3,500 per year. We suggest the purchase of an upgraded photocopier at a cost of $6,830 (this price includes maintenance for three years). This cost will be recovered in less than two years because of increased convenience and efficiency.

Details: *[Include estimates of delay and subsequent cost to the company; a summary of maintenance over the past two years, showing frequency and hours of downtime; samples of copy quality for the machine in use and for the model proposed for purchase; and a summary of the growth in employees on the third floor. Also include terms of the maintenance agreement for the proposed purchase.]*

A good report is clear and direct, draws and presents a conclusion, and gives the reader answers or at least ideas. These characteristics are what ultimately distinguish passive, unread reports from active, useful reports. To achieve that difference, you must start by knowing why the report is being written and anticipating the questions the reader needs answered. Let those thoughts guide you, and your reports will become valuable sources for information.

WORK PROJECT

1. You are asked to prepare a report showing the current status of projects underway. Several are running late. Before starting on this report, what questions do you anticipate the reader needs answered?

2. You want to write a report requesting more floor space for your department. What questions must you answer to define the purpose of the report?

3. Your boss asks for a report on maintenance costs for office equipment in your department. You are asked to include money spent, frequency of repairs, and hours machines have been inoperative in recent months. Your boss states that it might be time to trade in some older machines. Considering the request, what information should your report include?

2

The Format for Good Reports

"The food in this place is really terrible . . . and such small portions."

—Woody Allen

After the senior vice president saw the monthly status report, he wrote a memo to the manager who prepared it. The memo read, "Frankly, I found the format confusing and difficult to follow and I doubt whether I could use any of the information. Please be sure to put my name on your permanent distribution list, as I look forward to seeing the report each month."

Where and how do you learn the techniques for writing reports? They can't be taught in school, because every situation in your company is different and may require a specialized report. The best education you can get is on the job. But that brings up more problems: Most reports do not answer the right questions and most of us are never taught how to write them properly.

Too often reports are prepared without proper organization—the most important information is buried in the middle of the report or even placed on the last page, and related facts and figures are spread randomly throughout. In many cases, the recipient cannot even find the information needed, must less understand it.

THE PROPER ORGANIZATION OF REPORTS

Your final conclusion should be at the very front of the report. Most people simply don't have the time or the inclination to read a lengthy document. They are looking for the bottom line, your conclusion, or the one detail they must have right away. Yet, most reports are organized in the order in which the material was gathered and studied, so the reader must wade through many pages of preliminaries. Present your conclusions first and then back them up with the rest of the report.

Immediately following your summary, make recommendations. If some action is required, you should point it out here. Whenever possible, give the reader several choices and discuss the relative merit of each.

After the summary and recommendations, include any detailed, supporting information you need. If a reader questions your summary or recommendations, he or she can check your findings without having to come back and ask for more information.

One employee was asked to summarize the sales division's production for the month. She started with a summary of the most important information she had discovered and then listed appropriate recommendations:

Summary
    Overall production is behind forecasts by 11 percent. Three of the five divisions contribute to this variance:

Midwest	−23%
Southwest	−6%
Pacific	−14%

These unfavorable variances are offset by production in the remaining two divisions that exceeded forecasts:

East	+18%
South	+9%

An analysis of production this year and in the past reveals that:

1. Sales representatives who have been with the company

less than one year are producing substantially lower volume than had been forecast.

2. Remote divisions have historically fallen behind productivity rates in divisions closer to the home office.

3. Turnover rates among salespeople in divisions reporting unfavorable variances are significantly higher than the rates in the East and South divisions.

<u>Recommendations</u>

The unfavorable variance in sales volume may be resolved by coordinating marketing supervision efforts in the following ways:

1. Improve product and service training for new salespeople.

2. Conduct orientation and sales technique seminars for newly hired salespeople.

3. Perform closer home office supervision, monitoring, and goal enforcement with remote divisions.

4. Conduct a study of the causes of high turnover rates in remote divisions, including an analysis of screening and training techniques and the quality of sales support by division management.

5. Establish income goals for each division and for each salesperson, on the basis of assumptions included in the original income forecast.

6. Monitor closely the goals of those divisions reporting unfavorable variances.

Following the recommendations was a detailed summary of production in each division compared with the income forecast.

With this report, marketing management was able to quickly identify the problem by location and then direct its efforts toward solving that problem. The recommendations section indicated several steps that could be taken to improve the poor results and to improve productivity for the entire company.

The report could have been prepared by passively listing actual production by division compared to the original forecast. But that forces the reader to interpret the facts and come up with his or her own recommendations. With the proper format, you provide answers to solve problems, rather than simply listing data.

PRACTICAL APPLICATION OF THE FORMAT

You may have to prepare a long-established monthly or quarterly report that has an accepted, traditional format. By making changes that place important information where it can be found easily, you will be able to refocus your reports so that they provide information that the reader needs:

Example: In one research company, a newly hired employee is assigned a monthly report on the status of ongoing projects. The report is intended to show which jobs are on schedule, which ones are behind schedule, and which deadlines are upcoming. But the old format is a wordy narrative discussing the nature of each project at length, followed by a rambling summary of the status. The first section provides the same information each month, except when completed projects drop off the report and when new ones are added.

The employee sees that the report is difficult to read. It did not present important information up front or include a summary. She wants to recommend a change and decides the best way to do that would be to go ahead and prepare the report in a better format. She makes the following changes:

1. She begins the report with a chart summarizing ongoing projects. The chart shows the project deadline and progress to date on a time line, so that a reader can see at a glance where problems exist.
2. The second section explains the status of each project, concentrating on the problems that existed at that time. If a project is on schedule, she attempts to anticipate any upcoming scheduling problems.
3. The third section summarizes projects recently completed, including whether or not the deadline is met. If it isn't, an explanation is included.
4. The final section has narrative descriptions, but only of projects added that month. Reference is made to a separate project summary, a permanent file with details of current project.

The information a reader needs to review the current month's status is included in the report, but project descriptions are not repeated after their first appearance. These changes reduced the size of the report from over 70 pages to approximately 20 pages. The new format is accepted and made permanent.

It is not always that simple to make changes. As a rule, people resist new formats of reports or anything that alters the status quo. But if your ideas are sensible, if they make a report easier to read and use, and if they quickly summarize and clarify the information the reader wants, your ideas should be readily accepted.

FORMAT DICTATED BY NEED

The suggested format for internal reports—starting with the summary and placing details in the back—is appropriate when creating a new report or when an old report needs revising. Some types of reports, though, should not be treated in this way. They either require a straightforward communication of facts or they must be arranged according to particular rules. Some examples follow:

- You are asked to prepare a summary of financial information. Interpretation or comment is not required. The best format is a simple listing.
- A government agency requires that a report be written following a strict outline. There is no room for flexibility or alternative formats.
- In some industries, certain reports follow a prescribed order. Because everyone in that industry is accustomed to these reports, change is not practical.

However, you shouldn't apply a single standard to all reports. Frequently a format from one report is used for another, when an entirely new one should be devised. Part of the reason for this is habit. It's much easier to stay with a tried and true format, even when something else makes more sense.

In one firm, this practice created a problem. An internal report was done each month summarizing assignments of staff engineers. The report was especially difficult to follow, even though it could have been a very brief and specific report. The format was lengthy, it had excessive narrative sections, and rather than showing the level of commitment for each person, it reported data by job.

The chief engineer wanted to change the format, so he spoke to the manager responsible for its preparation. It turned out that the report was based on the same format that was used for producing job specifications. In that document, each type of material—wood, steel, glass, and so forth—was broken down by section and explained in great detail, ending with a complete materials list. In order to bid the job, the materials list was broken down by cost. This was the accepted format for that type of document, used by all engineering firms. In the report on staff commitment, a similar level of detail was provided—lengthy explanation was given by job, including possible future requirements and hours, ending with a summary of the original schedule and current status. In this case, a format appropriate for one type of report was completely wrong for another. You can overcome this natural resistance to change by demonstrating that revising the format of certain reports will make them easier to comprehend.

Even the simplest reports can be unclear if the wrong format is used. The president of an insurance company requests a monthly summary of new business, including insurance in force (face amounts of policies sold), premium earnings for new and existing business, cash received, and net profit. The first report reads as follows:

New Business Summary

The company reported an increase in new business in force for the month of January, totaling $17.35 million. This is net of lapsed and terminated policies.

As of Januray 31, total business in force totals $845.61 million.

During the same period, new business earned premiums totaled $42,860, and earned premiums from existing policies totaled $418,006.

Cash receipts were $331,882. The difference between earned premiums and cash received represents deferred payments on policies with varying anniversary dates and quarterly, semiannual, or annual payment schedules.

> January net profits (on an unaudited basis) were $63,018 from
> insurance operations, and $81,458 from net investment income.

This one-page report gives the president everything that he asked for, but in the wrong format. He didn't request interpretations or narrative explanations. For example, it should be assumed that the president understands why earned premiums are always different from cash received, and that monthly profit reports are not audited. If you establish a precedent for a poor format, it will be difficult to make changes later. It will also be tedious for the reader to get information from the report.

This report requires no recommendations or conclusions. All that was requested was a summary of information. A revised format of the report might look like this:

[*Revised*]

New Business Summary
January

New business this month	$ 17.35 million
Total business in force	$845.61 million
Earned premiums	
New business	$ 42,860
Existing business	418,006
Total earned	$460,866
Cash received	$331,882
Net profits	
Insurance	$ 63,018
Investments	81,458
Total net	$144,476

Format is not a difficult problem to resolve. Let the nature of the report's contents dictate the method of presentation. You should quickly communicate the most important facts or conclusions in the easiest way possible. You should always offer the best solutions possible when you explain problems. Always answer the reader's most important questions.

Apply these rules consistently and you will be recognized as a capable preparer of reports.

WORK PROJECT

1. An employee in your department has prepared a report for you. The summary is on the last page and recommendations are scattered throughout the report. What suggestions should you make for improving the format, and what reasons should you give for those changes?

2. The accounting manager has asked you to prepare a monthly summary of expenses committed to but not yet paid for by your department. This report is needed by the first of each month and will be used to prepare financial statements. What is the best format?

3. You take over responsibility for preparation of a monthy report that has been done every month for the last three years, and you have ideas for improving its format. How should you proceed in getting your ideas approved?

3

Segmenting the Process

"Begin at the beginning . . . and go till you come to the end; then stop."

—Lewis Carroll, *Alice's Adventures in Wonderland*

"I'm having a lot of trouble with the report I'm supposed to write," Marilyn told Cathy over lunch. Cathy suggested she should just start at the beginning and go through the job methodically. Marilyn asked, "How can I find the beginning when I'm still bogged down in the middle?"

When you have a big report to write, the task can look so formidable that you don't know where to begin. That's why many reports come in late or in a poorly organized format. But there's a simple way to manage a big project: Break it down into smaller projects and assign deadlines to each one. You read a book one chapter at a time, and a large job is a lot easier if it's done one step at a time.

IDENTIFYING PHASES

A simple report involves identifying specific information and selecting the best format to communicate it. But a more complex report involves a mixture of facts, trends, historical information, projections, and interpretation. When you're faced with the task of preparing a complicated report, a different approach is needed.

Every report can be broken down into phases, and each phase completed in turn. For a number of reasons, you will be better organized and more able to complete your report when using this approach (see "Advantages of Identifying Phases.")

Advantages of Identifying Phases

1. It will be easier to organize your material if you recognize the logical steps necessary to complete a report by deadline.
2. You avoid problems that might arise if the report is completed in the wrong order.
3. The delegation process is aided because tasks are isolated in small, well-focused areas.
4. The entire job is less overwhelming.
5. It's easier to work with people in other departments when the report is broken up. A smaller, narrowly focused phase is easier to complete than a complicated project with many parts.
6. Different phases can proceed at the same time when one doesn't depend on the other, making the deadline more manageable.
7. Phasing often helps you decide the best format for your report. Your original plan might change as you organize the phases, so that a more logical format emerges.

Your first task is to identify the logical phases that are involved in the project. In one financial services company, the president asked for a report on the time and cost involved in automating the entire office. He wanted the report within two months. The systems manager broke the task down into these phases:

1. *Definitions.* Some routines would not lend themselves well to automation, so specific areas to be automated must first be identified. This phase was based on interviews with all managers and supervisors in the company, as well as on discussions with the president at the time the assignment was made.

2. *Interdepartmental flow.*   All work done in any one department would affect work in another, so a complete system had to be organized with this in mind. This phase summarized the flow and discussed the routines and deadlines involved.

3. *Transaction summaries.*   This is a summary of the work volume for each of the areas of responsibility to be automated. To understand this, the systems manager had to interview each supervisor for each task and then predict future transaction loads.

4. *Program estimates.*   Initial estimates of the programming that would be involved in the conversion. These were based on interviews with computer systems resource people and an evaluation of existing software the company could purchase.

5. *Time analysis.*   A study of the time that would be required—combining inside and outside work—to develop the full system.

6. *Cost analysis.*   This was a preliminary budget based on discussions with outside software consultants and hardware manufacturers, as well as the systems manager's direct experience in conversions.

7. *Report preparation.*   The manager put the information into an appropriate format: first summarizing findings and making recommendations, then compiling supporting documents in a logical order.

This was a demanding project, involving a great deal of research. And unlike a historical or status report dealing only in facts, a lot of the work and conclusions depended upon projecting an unknown: the actual cost and time involved in converting from manual to automated systems.

The systems manager had these concerns as he began work on the project:

- An estimate of today's transaction level might not be relevant by the time a full system was designed and put into place.
- Any change in reporting requirements could make a system designed today obsolete a year later.
- Estimates of cost would be based on today's rates and might be much different later.
- Identifying the time involved to convert would depend upon several variable assumptions. If any one of these were wrong, the estimate would be inaccurate.

The manager included in his projections of time and cost enough latitude to allow for those variables. By tackling each phase in turn (with the entire task in mind, of course), he was able to prepare a detailed report by the assigned deadline. The variables were clearly discussed in the report, so that no one could get the impression that the conclusions were absolute. Defining and identifying phases is essential to good organization in your report. Some people will argue that the phases of a report cannot always be identified so easily and that therefore phasing is not a practical way to approach the reporting process. But, in fact, you must be able to identify the phases before you can solve any problem. If you haven't defined the elements of your task, you can't understand the problem and you can't write a meaningful report that presents solutions. This is true whether your report is simple or complex. And the greater the complexity of a report, the more definition and organization you need.

THE PROJECT SCHEDULE

Once you have broken your report into logical phases, the next step is to assign deadlines. This is necessary if you're doing the report on your own (to properly manage the time commitment needed to complete the report) or with the participation of others (to organize and control each phase as part of an overall deadline).

In the case of the study for the conversion, the manager identified seven phases. It was obvious that these phases did not have to proceed consecutively. In some instances, different phases could be worked on concurrently. For example, phases two and three (interdepartmental flow and transaction summary) were closely related and could be prepared at the same time. And phases four and five (program estimates and time analysis) were unrelated and did not depend upon each other. The two phases could proceed independently.

It was necessary to complete the first phase (definitions) before going on to anything else. And the second and third phases had to be finished before going beyond that point, because no estimates of program scope or time requirements could be made until the work load had been defined.

Figure 3-1.   Project schedule.

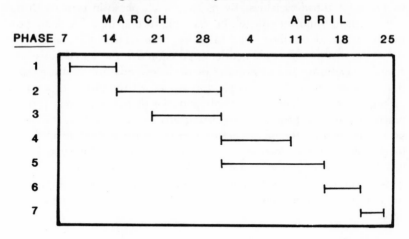

The manager came up with a project schedule, assigning deadlines to each phase of the report. This schedule is reproduced in Figure 3-1.

Here the concurrent opportunities can be seen and understood easily. Several people besides the manager were involved in the preparation of this report, so that good organization and control of deadlines were required to control the research and investigative phases. And whenever one phase could overlap another, more flexibility could be gained.

You must understand that a report can take more time than you have allowed. This may be because other people delay supplying you with what you need, or subordinates fail to finish assigned work on time, or your own schedule is limited. When estimating the time required to finish a report, realize that the best of plans can go wrong. Remember the following:

- People usually need more time to complete a job than you give them.
- You might not complete a phase by your own deadline, due to circumstances beyond your control.

- Good organization reduces the frequency of missing a deadline, but you still cannot expect a schedule to always work out.

CHECKING ON STATUS

One person must take primary responsibility for the completion of a large report. If that's you, be prepared to spend time checking the status of phases as the job proceeds.

The scheduling work you do is only useful if you use it to control the process. In the case of the systems manager's report on automating the office, he had to keep track of each phase from week to week. After he had completed the definitions, he needed information from other department managers for the second and third phases. Inevitably, when you depend on a number of other people, some of them will fail to meet your deadline. The systems manager allowed more than two weeks to gather information in these two phases. Aware that the report could not proceed until these phases were complete, he checked with each manager during the two weeks to ensure that work was proceeding.

He also devised a status summary for his own use. He tracked the progress in defining interdepartmental flow and transaction work load for each task. The two managers who had not started on their part of the job after one full week were reminded of the importance of the deadline. They were a bit late with their results, but anticipating this, the systems manager was still able to catch up and complete the report on time.

A simplified status worksheet is shown in Figure 3-2. The actual degree of completion is shaded in as the work is done. At any given date, you can see at a glance how well work is proceeding. This technique is especially useful when you must depend on other people. For example, the systems manager knew that he was depending on six different people to supply essential information. For the second and third phases of his project, which involved the most people, he used a status worksheet for each department.

Making up status worksheets for each department is a further

Figure 3-2. Checking status.

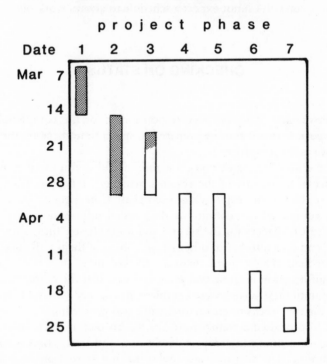

down of the phasing approach as described. Within any single phase, the task may have to be broken down by individual. Go into as much detail as you need to achieve the deadline and stay in control.

GIVING ASSIGNMENTS TO OTHERS

A report that depends on other people's efforts is likely to miss the deadline. It only takes one or two people failing to come through to hold up the entire project. To avoid delays, you must be able to give assignments and ensure that people follow through with their commitments.

Make sure that everyone involved understands the nature of the report. For example, the systems manager approaches the supervisor of a department and asks for a summary of transaction load. If the supervisor is not told why the request is made, he might think it's unimportant and postpone responding, or he might even feel threatened by the inquiry from outside his department. Failure to respond could result from lack of knowledge or from fear.

But if you explain the purpose thoroughly, the other person is more likely to respond. The systems manager explains that he is working on a report for the president of the company about the time and cost involved with automating various departments. He explains that as part of that study, it is necessary to identify work flow and transaction loads for each department. The supervisor now understands the reason for the request and is not afraid that the information will somehow threaten the department's security. Of course, automation (or whatever the purpose of your report is) can in itself be seen as a threat, but someone is more likely to respond when you take the time to explain not only what you need, but *why* you need it.

An advantage of the phasing technique is that it allows you to set preliminary deadlines. If the systems manager tells each manager on March 1st, "I have to have this report finished by the end of April," he is not going to get a quick response. The other managers assume that they can gather the information requested any time within the next few weeks.

Instead, the systems manager says: "I've been given only a few weeks to pull together all of this information. I can't do a time and cost analysis until I know about your work flow and transaction load. So I need you to give me your numbers no later than the end of March."

Diplomacy and communication combined with a little prodding will get better results from peers and subordinates. But how do you proceed when you need information from someone above you in rank?

In researching the conversion report, the systems manager has to check back with the president during the first phase, defining the scope of the conversion. He has concluded that some routines should not be included in the job, but, before proceeding with that assumption, he wants verification from the top. So he asks for a meeting.

The president hears his arguments and says, "I want to think about this. Let's get together again at the end of the week." The following day, the president has to cancel the meeting, and is planning to be out of town the entire week after that. The systems manager tells him, "I can't proceed until I'm sure of the scope you intended. If we delay our meeting a week, I'll have to ask for a week's delay in the deadline for the report. Is that all right?"

This is a diplomatic way of forcing the president to adjust his request, or to make room in his schedule to finalize the definition phase. In this case, the president meets with the systems manager that same week. The problem is resolved in less than 10 minutes and the project proceeds on schedule.

A long report involving a lot of research and time on your part should provide exactly what the reader asks for. But in some cases, your understanding of the request will not be what is actually needed or wanted. So it's a good idea to meet with that person during your definition phase and make sure that you're proceeding in the right direction.

COORDINATING ASSIGNMENTS

If a single report assignment is so complex that it requires widespread participation, develop a well-defined schedule for completion of the phases. This requires comprehensive review and analysis in the definition phase and perhaps a flowchart of the sequence and interaction required to get the report done.

The weakest link in the progress of a team effort report is any person outside of your immediate and direct control—someone in another department or even outside the company. As long as you are working on your own or with people who report directly to you, deadlines are easily enforced. But when you depend on someone else, be sure you explain their role in the overall report.

In especially complex situations, a flowchart of the phases and participation might be needed. The purpose of the flowchart is to identify the weak links in your schedule so that you know where to put the extra effort to ensure that deadlines are met.

With a flowchart, you will be able to see at a glance exactly how each step fits into the process. Design flowcharts that not only identify steps, but the departments involved as well. This method not only identifies weak links, but also points out potential for communication breakdowns. Whenever a procedure moves from one department to another, there may be miscommunication. For example, a procedure includes seven steps. The flowchart identifies each step in order, from top to bottom; it also shows where the work is done:

Department A	Department B	Department C
Step 1		
Step 2		
	Step 3	
Step 4		
Step 5		
		Step 6
Step 7		

The weak links are steps 3 and 6, because they are done outside of your direct control and you cannot set a deadline as effectively as you can in your own area of authority. You should communicate very specifically how work is to be done and when it must be completed when the project moves from one department to another.

REPORTING ON STATUS

If you need several weeks to prepare a report, it's a good idea to meet with the manager or executive who requested the report while you're working on it.

You will encounter problems of delegation when your report requires a collective effort. When you are working on a large report all by yourself, you can still run into problems with deadlines.

Example: A manager in a marketing company is assigned to write a procedures manual for several departments. He breaks the project down into definition and resource phases, and outlines the sections of the manual. He also requests periodic meetings with his boss and the executive vice president to review progress. This achieves two objectives:

It ensures that the work is in line with the request and enables him to get help, if needed, in obtaining information from other departments.

Several problems do arise. The manager needs help from other departments and the information does not always come in according to schedule. The manager has to do without some essential information and go on to other parts of the manual in order to stay on schedule. He also asks for help from the executive vice president in getting some information from outside departments, realizing he doesn't have the rank to insist on compliance in every case.

A multiphase project can often be scheduled with flexibility, so that you don't have to delay completion because someone else is not coming through. Manage your own time as efficiently as possible. When you initiate a schedule that will depend on others, ask for information earlier than you need it. It's better to receive some data well in advance of your deadline than to end up sitting on your hands because someone else is late.

Communicate regularly on two levels. First, stay in touch with those in other departments from whom you need information. Let them know your deadlines and check periodically to remind them of the help you need. Second, meet with the individual expecting the final report and give them a status report. If you anticipate a delay, be prepared to explain why. For each phase of the project, use a brief status report like the one shown in Figure 3-3.

Anyone can quickly see where each phase stands in this status report. In the "completion" section, shade in the level of progress to the appropriate point. For example, you give two weeks for the completion of one phase in a project. You divide the "date" section into five groups of three days each. When you complete the status report, you have less than a week until scheduled completion, but the project is only 40 percent done. This might indicate a problem, unless you know the remaining work can be completed by the end of the week. You include explanations in the "notes" section.

By reviewing the status of each phase in a report project, a reader can quickly see how the report is proceeding. If, for example, you come to the conclusion that the report will not be completed by the requested date, you should communicate this as quickly as possible. Some others might be depending on getting that report, and they should know right

Figure 3-3.   Status report.

status report

Report _____

Phase _____

Today's date _____ **Deadline** _____

D A T E S

start ____   ____   ____   ____   ____   ____ finish

c o m p l e t i o n

Notes _____

_____

_____

_____

_____

_____

_____

_____

_____

_____

away if it isn't going to be on time. When you are not able to deliver on time, document the reasons.

By using the phasing system, you will be able to deliver reports on time and, occasionally, *early*. Strive to stay ahead of your own deadlines, and be sure to build flexibility into the schedule. If you use this procedure, you will be recognized as a dependable employee who responds to and meets deadlines.

WORK PROJECT

1. Your company is considering publishing a newsletter for employees. Your assignment is to prepare a report summarizing the cost of producing the newsletter. What are the phases of the report?

2. While mapping out a report, you estimate the time required to complete each phase. It looks like you will be able to deliver the final version two weeks ahead of schedule. Should you promise the report early?

3. The assignment you've been given is especially complicated and will require a good deal of time to complete. How can you ensure that you will be proceeding correctly?

4

The Narrative Form

A newly hired employee couldn't understand the section of the company's operating manual that explained how to prepare reports. The opening paragraph read, "In a written communications mode, it is a preparatory responsibility to avoid obfuscation." The employee asked his manager what that meant, and the manager replied, "It says to write reports clearly and simply."

Many reports are written in the strictly narrative form, which means that a series of facts is presented with the use of words alone. There are no charts or graphs that break up or simplify an explanation. And financial information is given within the context of a paragraph.

Writing reports in a strict narrative format can be tricky. How often have you seen reports that are virtually unreadable? They are poorly organized, unclear, and are difficult to distinguish from the same report of the month before. The point of the report—if there is one—is lost in rambling text that puts the reader to sleep before he or she can make sense out of it.

As discussed previously, how you organize the report can go a long way toward eliminating these common problems. A summary (consisting of a cover memo and introductory material) explains exactly what the report contains. A recommendations section gives the reader the conclusions and key points in the report. And support material (often the body of the report itself) supplies additional information that should lead to action.

However, even the best format does not ensure that the report will be read and well received. For that to happen, you need to make the report both informative and interesting.

CONSTRUCTING A NARRATIVE REPORT

A report's success might not depend on visual aids or long columns of numbers, which break up the test. A narrative can still be clear and interesting.

The first draft of a report on quarterly revenue by division started with this summary section:

> For the second quarter, the Eastern Division reported revenues of $835,600, a 19% increase over the previous quarter. The Southern Division reported $519,400, a 10% increase. Midwest Division had $415,500, a decrease of 3%. And the Pacific Division reported $404,200, a decrease of 1% from the previous quarter.

That is certainly not interesting reading. In a narrative report, financial information—especially when it's as repetitive as this—can be summarized and put into a much more readable form. Remember that the reader needs the facts at a glance, and the most important facts should be given first. Consider the following redraft of the report:

[Revised]

> Revenues for the quarter grew by 8.2% overall. As in previous quarters, gains in Eastern and Southern divisions were responsible for this growth, while Midwest and Pacific divisions reported continuing reductions:

Eastern	$835,600	+19%
Southern	519,400	+10
Midwest	415,500	− 3
Pacific	404,200	− 1

This is still considered a narrative report, since the financial summary is not displayed separately. The information is a part of the paragraph, but it is presented in a more understandable form in approximately the same amount of space as in the first draft. Not only that, but the important increase in revenues overall is reported up front. That these revenue changes are a continuing trend is also mentioned in the short paragraph. The paragraph closes with the actual numbers and percentage breakdowns in summary.

When you are faced with reporting a number of facts, take the reader's point of view. Assume that you need the information, and that you want it in order of priority. You key on the most important facts and highlight them, and perhaps even include the conclusion the reader should draw. After that, back up your report with the details.

MAKING THE REPORT READABLE

When you begin constructing the report, you may be overwhelmed by the volume of information. But if you take a methodical and organized approach, you will construct a readable and informative report.

One manager in an internal auditing department is given the task of writing procedures for creating and maintaining employee task descriptions. The purpose of this assignment is to ensure that all task descriptions conform to internal auditing standards and satisfy control measures in all sections of the company.

The manager meets with employees and supervisors and designs procedures to monitor task descriptions and to update them. He organizes his procedures in an outline. Unlike most reports, a procedures manual usually has a unique format. As a specialized reporting form, it should be practical for the employee executing a procedure and should also help supervisors to ensure that the proper method is being followed. Because the procedures for this company are especially long, the manager includes a table of contents:

The material is straightforwardly organized and presented in each section. This makes a rather complex subject simple. It is broken down into steps, and each section deals with only one subject.

Some of the formatting techniques used in this case are shown in Figure 4–1. The letters indicate the following:

A. Each page includes a one-word title and page number at the top. With this, the reader can tell at any point what section of the report is being reviewed.
B. Each section starts out with a brief statement of what is included.
C. Other relevant sections of the report are cross-referenced.
D. The outline form is used to explain steps.

This report can be read once and understood. The outline format enables you to list exactly what happens as you go through a process. The simplified description of the supervisor's review is precise and to the point. And the outline format is superior to the description in paragraph form.

> Each department's supervisor reviews the task descriptions prepared by each employee. This review takes place once per month and looks at validity under current procedures, clarity, inclusion of sample forms and worksheets, a work-flow summary, and deadlines.

To a reader unfamiliar with the review process, this paragraph is confusing. When you use that format throughout a 30-page report, it will be very difficult for the reader to gain information.

USING CROSS-REFERENCES

Another way to make narrative reports as clear as possible is to make the reader's task easy by cross-referencing thoroughly. This is especially true in long reports, where a statement or conclusion is supported by more detailed information found elsewhere.

Figure 4-1.   Formatting techniques.

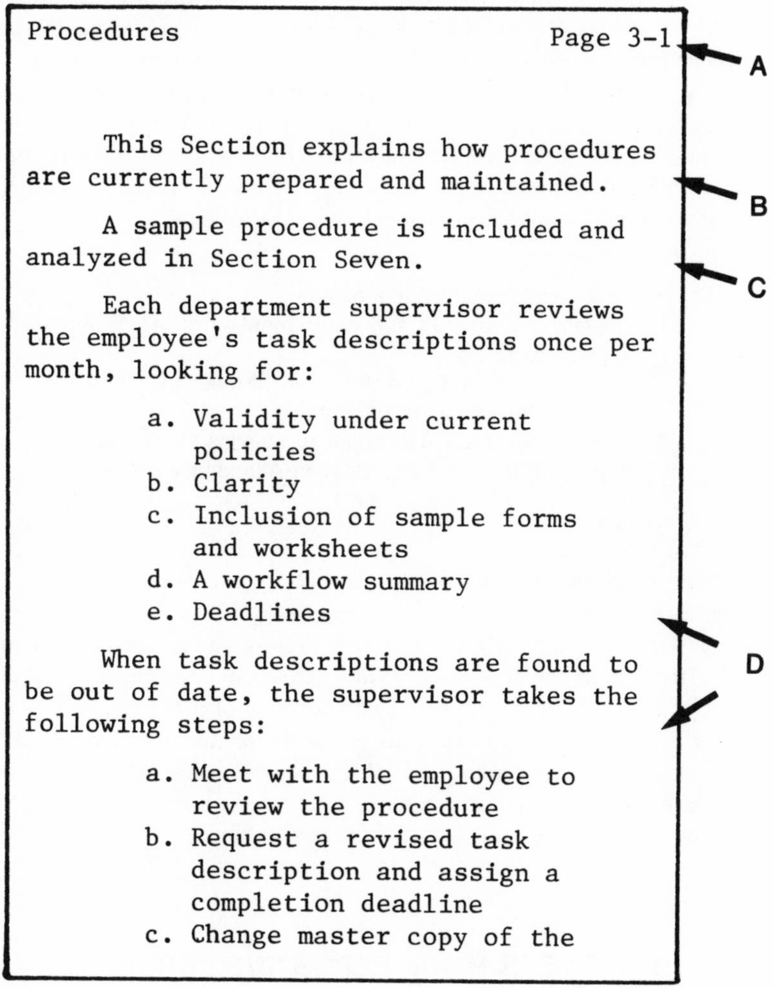

```
Procedures                          Page 3-1
```
                                                              ← A

     This Section explains how procedures
are currently prepared and maintained.
                                                              ← B
     A sample procedure is included and
analyzed in Section Seven.
                                                              ← C
     Each department supervisor reviews
the employee's task descriptions once per
month, looking for:

          a. Validity under current
             policies
          b. Clarity
          c. Inclusion of sample forms
             and worksheets
          d. A workflow summary
          e. Deadlines

     When task descriptions are found to   D
be out of date, the supervisor takes the
following steps:

          a. Meet with the employee to
             review the procedure
          b. Request a revised task
             description and assign a
             completion deadline
          c. Change master copy of the

In your recommendations section, cross-reference each major point to the appropriate supporting information, including the page number and title of the section. And if you mention key findings or qualifiers in your summary, cross-reference that to the recommendations section.

A good rule to follow is this: Any statement or conclusion you make, or any mention of financial information, should be cross-referenced so that the reader has no questions about where your facts come from or what they mean. An example of a cross-referenced recommendations section of a report on internal meetings follows:

> The following recommendations are made:
>   1. Prepare an agenda for each meeting. (See Sample Agenda, page 4-6.)
>   2. Set strict start and stop times for all meetings. (See the Study of Meeting Costs, page 4-9.)
>   3. Limit attendance. (See proposed Meeting Procedures on page 4-17 and Analysis, Meeting Attendance on page 4-20.)

Using cross-references establishes a sense of organization in your report. It shows that you have put thought into the order of presentation and that you know the subject well enough to present key issues up front and details later on in the report. The alternative, and the more common format of doing reports, is to start out with a lot of detail.

In the typical report, the details disorient the reader and do not lead to solid conclusions. The reader has to search for the meaning of the report. And since most reports are passive and don't have conclusions or recommendations, the mass of detail is not significant.

THE FIVE COMMON REPORTING ERRORS

Make your reporting excellent by identifying the most common pitfalls and avoiding them. Regardless of the business your company is in, the following errors are universal.

Failing to Orient the Reader

Remember that the reader is not as familiar with the material as you are. Too many reports jump right into an explanation without reminding the reader what the report is about.

You should start out by explaining that the report has a specific purpose. And it doesn't hurt to mention the purpose several times in the context of a detailed discussion. Also relate each section to the report as a whole, so that it is in context for the reader. For example, in one company any report of five pages or more always includes a table of contents. One report identified sections as follows:

Overwriting the Report

Some reports can be vastly improved by editing. The tendency to overwrite should always be avoided, because a brief but informative report is preferable to one that goes on too long about more information than anyone needs.

There is nothing wrong with simplicity. A report is only as interesting as it is understandable. The myth that reports should sound important or use longer words than necessary is destructive. Here's an example of a poorly written statement:

> Evaluation of the success of the planned geographic expansion of markets to three additional states will present significant difficulties. Judgments concerning the intrinsic effectiveness of this strategic plan cannot be materialized during the first annual period, as anticipated market responsiveness to our marketing penetration efforts must be expected to materialize in gradual steps during the period in question.

This can be said much more clearly:

> The success of our three-state market plan will be hard to judge during the first year. Resistance of the market cannot be measured until a solid trend is established.

Read over the statements you write and look for a more direct way to express your message. Virtually every first draft can be improved with this simple step.

Making Weak Statements

Your reports should take a definite stand, make a statement, and communicate information directly. Out of fear that strong statements will be challenged, or just from lack of research, many reports hedge on facts.

A statement might be weak from unconscious habit, a problem that is easily and quickly solved by careful editing. But a more serious problem is the tendency to write to hide the *lack* of information. If you are uncertain about a point, don't try to write your way around it. Stop and look for answers. The following is an example of a poorly written statement concerning the need to increase a department's size during the next year:

> Our department will probably need to hire at least one and possibly two new employees in the near future.
> Work loads today are quite heavy, with employees able to complete assigned tasks but up against deadlines continuously. If that work load increases as we expect that it will, we will need additional help.

Notice how phrases like "will probably need" and "at least one and possibly two" are inprecise. With a little more research, the statement can be redrafted to present a definite conclusion. Here is an example of how it could be rewritten:

> Our department will need to hire one new employee by March 1, and another no later than August 1.

Work loads will increase due to regional market expansion, growth in volume and the number of customer accounts, and new assignments given to the department over the past year.

The average number of transactions processed was 950 per month last year, but is 1,400 now, an increase of 47%. There has been no increase in the number of employees in the department and we expect a 30% growth in transaction volume over the next 12 months.

Making Unclear Statements

Just as a weak statement is bad because it takes a lot of impact away from your report, an unclear statement is bad because it discourages the reader. Always make your statements as clear as possible.

For every subject you cover in your report, there is one central fact to highlight. You can avoid confusing the reader by identifying that central fact.

Confusing:
The department spent $415 for travel and entertainment during the month; $384 on delivery; $600 for equipment leases; and $87 for miscellaneous. For the month, the department shows an unfavorable variance of 6%, primarily caused by travel and entertainment expenses.

Clear:
Travel and entertainment expenses account for the majority of a 6% unfavorable variance for the month (summary attached).

Confusing:
New customer accounts in the Pacific region were 2,368 for the quarter, down from 2,531 in the previous quarter and down from 2,845 in the same quarter last year. This compares to overall growth of 11% for the company over the previous quarter, and 14% over the same quarter last year.

Clear:
The trend in the Pacific region continues negatively. Company-wide growth is up in comparison to the past:

to previous quarter	+11%
to previous year	+14%

The Pacific division reported 2,368 new customer accounts, compared:

to previous quarter	−6%
to previous year	−17%

Confusing:

The advertising budget was increased 28% for the last six months, compared with budgets for the six-month period preceeding. Revenues for the company were $1.37 million compared to $1.39 million in the previous six months.

Clear:

No immediate growth in revenues has resulted from a 28% increase in the advertising budget for the last six months.

Viewing Reports as Routine or Unimportant

If you think, "No one reads these reports, anyway," and your report is difficult to read or the critical information is not readily available on the first page, you can be certain that no one will read your reports. Don't rush through them or ignore the need for thoughtful format decisions. Highlight important information for the reader. Summarize, remind, and cross-reference your reports so that the report is absolutely essential to the reader.

The narrative report may be the most difficult of all forms to do well. It requires careful structure and you must be aware of reader interest. An especially long narrative report requires a lot of reading, so there's a tendency to skim. Be sure to include your key information in the front. If it's cross-referenced to other sections, the reader will gain the information you intend to pass on.

Compared with strictly financial forms, narrative reports tend to be long. But, as you will see in coming chapters, the use of narratives can make any format more interesting and informative.

WORK PROJECT

1. You are writing a report on budget variances for the month. You have the following information: Travel and entertainment expenses were

$4,587, $587 over budget; office supplies were $682, $50 over budget; postage expenses were $218, or $82 under budget; and printing was $832, $82 over budget. How would you write a narrative summary of the status in these accounts?

2. You are rewriting a report prepared by someone else that proposes that the company should purchase additional computer terminals. The original statement reads, "Acquisition of computer terminals is mandated by indicated workload growth trends in the department. During the past six months, customer transactions in-cresed from 1,135 during the average month to more than 1,500." How would you rewrite this statement?

3. You are working on a report explaining procedures in use for preparing to input information on a computer terminal. An employee writes the following description: "Input is done directly from invoices. First, the supervisor approves them for payment. Then, we check cross-footings and match them to a requisition. Then a code is assigned for each expense and, if necessary, it is broken down into all affected accounts. Then a batch total is added. This is used later to verify the total of all input." Rewrite this using an outline format.

5

The Financial Form

"A nap, my friend, is a brief period of sleep which overtakes superannuated persons when they endeavor to entertain unwelcome visitors or to listen to scientific lectures."

—George Bernard Shaw, *Back to Methuselah*

An accounting supervisor complained to his manager, "No one really reads my reports. It's the same old thing every month—financial condition, statistics, ratios, trends, all numbers. What can I do to make it more interesting?" After a moment, the manager responded, "I'm sorry, my mind was wandering. What were you saying?"

Here's a challenge for you. Write a report that consists primarily of numbers and make it so interesting that your reader can't put it down. You probably believe that when it comes to strictly financial reports you have little or no latitude. But that's not true. You can make a report interesting by the way you present the information. You should explain what the numbers mean, rather than simply compile a list of results.

DEVELOPING A STANDARD

A report that consists primarily of numbers is naturally dull. You must translate numbers into human terms and make the numbers illustrate actual facts that the reader can understand, use, and act upon.

For example, the manager of the accounts receivable department in one large corporation prepares a report each month that summarizes the status of outstanding accounts. This report goes to the vice president and is also used as a guide in collection procedures within the department. The manager lists customers by the number of days since due date.

Because business is seasonal, considerable variation exists during the year in the volume of accounts and in the time required to receive payment. The customers have their own seasons and resulting variations, and this is reflected in the trend in collections. So the manager decides the list doesn't tell the whole story. She compares trends over a three-year period and identifies a reasonable collection time by season. From this, she develops a running trend analysis to accompany the report. It shows three things:

1. A trend in the average number of days that accounts remain unpaid, by season.
2. A ratio between credit-based sales and outstanding receivables.
3. Changes in current versus past-due accounts for the month, with seasonal factors included.

With the trend analysis included, the manager's report is more valuable, both within and outside the department. She develops a standard, so that a reader can tell whether the current status of accounts is above or below that standard. Whenever it is below, either collection procedures are being relaxed or some outside factor is at work (for example, one large account may be unusually late in payment).

This new approach adds insight to your reports, making them valuable to the reader. As a result, your narrative conclusions are specific, leading to recommendations and action. Even a strictly financial report can be improved. As long as the reader can benefit from more information or from a change in format, you can achieve a lot working just with numbers.

For example, a monthly income statement is prepared by an office manager of a marketing company. The division vice president has asked for a breakdown of income, expenses, and net profits, all compared with the budget. The office manager thinks it would be more significant to compare this information with the previous year-to-date and prepares it that way. The division vice president reacts immediately, because the new report gives him so much more information. The monthly numbers alone had shown only what was happening now. But with the previous year's figures added in, he can see whether the level of profit is better or worse, whether the volume of sales is higher or lower, and he can compare every expense with the past year's expense to see if there's a trend.

If you compare current information with past data, you establish a standard for measurement. But be sure that the standard is consistent with what you report today. For example, one company includes postage, printing, and stationery in one account called Office Expenses. As business grows, they decide to break Office Expenses into three accounts. In doing a year-to-year comparison, it is necessary to restate either the current year's numbers or the past year's. That might mean a great deal of analysis of an entire year's records, but making the report accurate is worth the trouble. If restating a prior year's numbers is too great a task or impossible to do accurately, restate the current year or modify the format. For example:

Account	Prior Year	Current Year	Change
Postage		$ 293.16	
Printing	$5,124.80	2,344.80	$(492.83)
Stationery		1,994.01	

The reason many financial reports are uninteresting is because no standard for comparison exists. The reader won't express complete satisfaction with a report if the present status can't be compared with a standard. That doesn't mean that there must be an improvement (such as higher sales or lower expenses). A report can be interesting and useful because the information is valid. If a report shows that last year's performance was better, the reader learns that there's a need for corrective action. The report communicates information that someone can use.

The standard for comparison can consist of several factors, both historical and current. Besides comparing the current financial status with the prior year's status, you can compare one division with another. Some financial reporting can be done on the basis of generally accepted standards. For example, the current ratio (current assets divided by current liabilities) should be 2 to 1 or better in most cases. For companies that do not keep inventories, a quick assets ratio—the same computation—should produce a 1-to-1 or better result. In some industries, a specific percentage of net profit is considered "acceptable" or "normal." These are all possible standards for comparison in your report.

For example, a manager prepares a financial summary for a new company. There are no divisions and no previous history. So he compares the different factors of the summary to each other. He expresses each expense both in dollar value and as a percentage of gross revenues. The validity of this format is admittedly questionable, even though it is commonly used. For example, there is no direct connection between fixed overhead accounts, such as rent and sales. The value of percentage breakdowns without other comparisons is limited. Suppose that a monthly profit and loss statement compares each cost and expense to gross sales. Costs make up 61 percent of the gross sales, expenses make up 32 percent, and that leaves 7 percent as profit. This format is not comparative, but at least it gives the reader more than just the numbers.

CHOOSING A FORMAT

What can you do with a column of numbers? Actually, you can do quite a bit. You have the opportunity to add validity and develop the best possible format at the same time.

Most people report numbers in a few standard and unimaginative ways. But you should always question the purpose of the report. Who is the reader? What does he or she need to know? And what is the order or priority?

A basic financial statement usually consists of a list of accounts and the respective amounts. But what is the essential information the reader wants? Consider a summary/detail format for your report. In one company, the accounting manager puts together a companywide income statement each month. But it includes a very brief summary of key information, followed by subsidiary schedules. A separate section is included for notes and comments: footnotes to the financial statement, special circumstances, and ongoing trend summaries.

The key information section is on a single page:

Financial Summary

	Current Period	Increase (Decrease)	
		Last Month	Last Year
Gross Revenue	$862,300	(2.3%)	12.8%
Direct Costs	493,600	(2.6)	6.6
Gross Profit	$368,700	(2.0%)	22.3%
Expenses	285,100	2.1	(18.4)
Net Profit	$ 83,600	0.1%	3.9%

After this summary, the manager places subsidiary schedules. These include a traditional current-period income statement, breakdowns by division, and a detailed, comparative listing of expenses. An additional section includes notes and comments, such as a summary of significant trends, notes on forecasts and budgets, and a listing of special adjustments and any extraordinary items included on the statement.

This format gets rid of clutter, allowing you to put the most important information up front and then support it with other details in following sections.

Another format to consider is annotation. In most financial status reports, a list of numbers is given alone and qualifiers and comments are placed on another page. You can make the presentation of financial information more interesting and, often, more significant by annotating the list.

For example, your assignment is to list general expenses for the quarter. You are to note any unusual situations and highlight all major budget variances. One format would be to simply prepare a list and then write your notes on attached pages. But remembering that the reader will want to see everything of significance at a glance, there is an alternative. By annotating your major list, you draw attention to the important comments. More detail can be provided by way of supporting documents and worksheets. An example of the annotation format is shown in Figure 5-1.

Another way the same assignment could be handled is with footnotes. The point with either annotation or footnote formats is that the essential information is included on one page. In this way, the reader can get what he or she needs without having to turn pages to hunt for important facts. With footnotes you simply add a letter or number to the left or right of your financial information and explain your footnote on the bottom of the page.

Figure 5-1. Annotation.

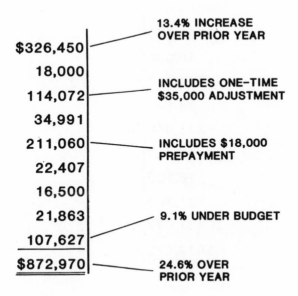

If you are listing account names followed by financial information, either include the footnote reference to the right of the number or to the right of the account name:

         Office supplies (1) $4,730
         Office supplies $4,730 (1)

The footnote format is shown in Figure 5-2.

HIGHLIGHTED FORM

Financial information can frequently be presented in a greatly summarized form. Depending upon who will get your report, you may not have to provide a lot of details, as long as the information the reader needs is available.

Figure 5-2. Footnotes.

$326,450	(A)
18,000	
114,072	(B)
34,991	
211,060	(C)
22,407	
16,500	
21,863	
107,627	(D)
$872,970	(E)

A. 13.4% INCREASE
OVER PRIOR YEAR

B. INCLUDES ONE-TIME
$35,000 ADJUSTMENT

C. INCLUDES $18,000
PREPAYMENT

D. 9.1% UNDER BUDGET

E. 24.6% OVER
PRIOR YEAR

For example, you are assigned the quarterly financial report, which includes income, breakdowns for four divisions, and comments on trends in sales and profits. In the past, this report was several pages long, with one page for the entire company and one page for each division.

There are several flaws with this traditional format. There is no summary of significant discoveries or trends, at least not until the reader gets to the comments section. Remembering that a report should contain key points up front, how can you conform to the reporting requirements of this assignment and still present valid, meaningful conclusions for the reader?

More seriously, the reader cannot compare performance by division with the traditional report. Since each division is discussed separately, the financial information is segregated. There may be significant trends or other conclusions that would be apparent if the information were on one page.

This format is also flawed because the comments section is removed from the financial details. So the reader has to page back and forth to piece together the validity of the comments.

The traditional format is also very passive. It is not designed to point out obvious trends and comparisons. It doesn't make drawing conclusions easy, so that no real action will follow the report. For example, how can the reader tell which divisions are more profitably run? It may be that two divisions account for most of the sales and yet receive a lower portion of expenses. This disparity might be mentioned in the comments section at the back of the report, when it should be mentioned up front.

When you must report on a variety of information in financial format, consider starting out with a summary of the highlights. What is significant about the numbers? What should the reader see on the first page?

Figure 5-3 shows how highlighted information can be presented on a single page. In this case, there are three significant facts to report:

1. There's an overall profit for the quarter of $234,512.
2. The East and South divisions account for 71 percent of all sales, but only 66 percent of total expenses.
3. Midwest and Pacific divisions represent 29 percent of sales, but 34 percent of expenses.

Figure 5-3.   Highlighted form.

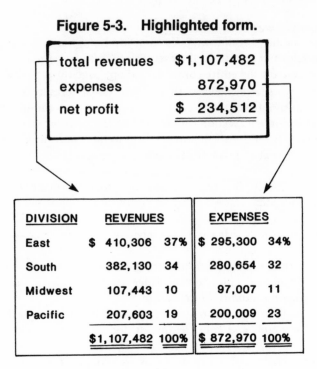

total revenues	$1,107,482	
expenses	872,970	
net profit	$ 234,512	

DIVISION	REVENUES		EXPENSES	
East	$ 410,306	37%	$ 295,300	34%
South	382,130	34	280,654	32
Midwest	107,443	10	97,007	11
Pacific	207,603	19	200,009	23
	$1,107,482	100%	$ 872,970	100%

SUGGESTING CHANGES

You will not always have the authority to change the format of a report. If that is the case, how can you suggest that changes be made? The best solution is to prepare the report in the improved format and submit it. If you suggest change without a sample, you are trying to win your case with no proof. If you simply submit the report in its new format, one of three things will happen:

  1. No one will comment on the change. In this case, you assume that either there are no problems with the new format or no one

bothered to read the report before. They might be embarrassed to admit that they didn't understand the report before your changes were made.

2. Your new format will be approved.
3. The change will be rejected and you will have to rewrite the report in the old format. This means more work, but it's better to try and be rejected than to passively go along when you know you could do better.

People fear change, even when that change is an obvious improvement. You may face considerable resistance to your ideas, especially if you offer only ideas without proof. The most convincing argument you can make for an improved format is going to be the report itself. Your boss may respond by saying, "I like the format, but the president is used to the old way of doing things." Then you should suggest a different approach. You can prepare the report using the improved format and attach a list pointing out the new format's advantages and the shortcomings of the previous format. Then ask for approval of the change.

You can also deal with resistance by adding to a report rather than changing it. For example, an accounting manager protests changing the traditional format of a financial statement because there's a universal, acceptable way to present that information. Your compromise is to present the traditional format as part of the report and for external distribution, but to rearrange information in another section along the lines of your new ideas. The traditional statement is included as an extra section at the end of the report or even on a page after your highlights section.

Every report can be improved in some way. Emphasize the validity of information and highlight key points and conclusions in the front of the report and then support it with other sections. Do not use formats that report significant findings in different sections, forcing the reader to go through the entire report to find all the important information. And use formats that make financial reports pleasing to the eye and easy to follow. You might not be able to make financial information exciting; but by following these guidelines, you can be certain that your reports will be read.

WORK PROJECT

1. You prepare a status report each month comparing total sales to sales for the previous month. For the latest month, sales are down by 14 percent of the month before. However, your company is going into its slow season and you see that this month's sales are more than 30 percent above sales for the same month last year. How would you suggest changing the format of this report?

2. You are writing a report on the feasibility of a project your company is considering. In previous reports, financial information was summarized in the front and comments followed. The last section summarized key points and made a specific recommendation. How would you suggest changing the report?

3. A report has been done for many years in the same way. It's uninteresting and does not take priorities into account or present information in a clear manner. You have recently taken over responsibility for the report and want to change the format. What arguments can you make in support of your ideas?

6
Graphics in Reports

"Over time even two armed blind men in a room can do enormous damage to each other, not to speak of the room."

—Henry Kissinger

"Use lines instead of dots," the manager instructed his employee. "We haven't been using graphs very long now, and I'm not sure some people understand their purpose." When the employee asked why lines were better, the manager explained, "Last time we sent this out using dots, one of our executives connected them."

Your recommendations will be favored more often when you include graphics in your reports. Experts agree that people get the vast majority of their information visually. Clarifying information with charts and graphs not only helps the reader grasp what you are saying, it also improves your ability to communicate complex ideas quickly and simply.

Attempting to explain a complex trend with words alone frequently means the reader misses the point altogether. But when the information is presented graphically, the underlying significance is apparent.

Charts and graphs can improve reader interest and comprehension, but they should be used with care. It's a mistake to use visual aids to excess or to reduce everything to visual form when narratives will work better. Just as the absence of charts and graphs makes a report dry and uninteresting, overuse will completely undercut their intended purpose.

THE SIMPLE CHART

The easiest graphic representation to make is the chart. A report may include a financial summary, for example, within text simply by breaking the format. The distinction between a chart and a table depends on how these terms are used in your company. In general terms, a table is a narrative summary set off from the text. A chart is further distinguished by being boxed or bordered by lines above and below. The table is acceptable, but making it into a graphic gives your report more flavor, and has several advantages:

1. It breaks up the monotony of a continuous narrative report.
2. Simply putting a box around part of your report draws attention to the information, highlighting its significance.
3. A chart orients the reader. By referring to the chart, a related narrative section makes more sense and improves comprehension.

The chart is easy to prepare. It can be included within text or on a page by itself, depending upon its size and whether or not it fits within the text of the narrative.

Be sure the title is short but precise. The reader should not have any doubt what the chart shows. To prepare a chart, convert information to a columnar or tabular form and identify rows and columns. Lines are drawn above and below the material or it is boxed to emphasize the chart and set it apart from text.

For example, your first draft includes the following narrative explanation:

The department currently includes 16 employees, up from 11 employees in the third quarter; nine in the second quarter; and four in the first quarter.

Your report will be easier to read if you save narratives for discussion and reduce this information to chart form:

Number of Employees	
1st quarter	4
2nd quarter	9
3rd quarter	11
4th quarter	16

A chart can summarize information that can take hundreds of words to explain narratively. A chart usually means instant understanding, and the information is also retained and appreciated to a greater extent than if it has been reported in a narrative. Following is an example of a chart set off in a box.

Revenues, first quarter	$487,600
Revenues, prior quarter	$401,100
Increase	21.6%

This technique can also be used for nonfinancial information. For example, you are working on a report discussing the value of internal controls to prevent pilferage and you want to highlight certain information. Your report could be set up using the highlighting technique:

> Installing a cash-control procedure will ultimately prevent pilferage. In one study, the conclusion was reached that the act of putting controls into effect has a direct and immediate impact. That study revealed:

> - Pilferage is reduced immediately in response to announcing upcoming control procedures.
> - Employees are less likely to take supplies when they believe the company is monitoring.

Also use the chart as a technique for reporting information that doesn't fit the flow of your report but that you want to include. For example, you are discussing revenue forecasts and want to include a two-paragraph section on internal forecasting procedures. That's off the subject, but relates to solving the problem the company has in making its forecasts. Set the two-paragraph segment off by itself and draw lines around it. This creates a sidebar within your report—a form of chart that adds variety, keeps your flow consistent, and gives the reader extra information that might be missed if placed in a separate section.

TYPES OF GRAPHS

Charts are effective, easy-to-use tools for summarizing information in reports. You can also add variety and clarity by drafting simple graphs. There are four broad categories of graphs:

1. Vertical bar graph
2. Horizontal bar graph
3. Line graph
4. Circle graph

Each of these graphs is best suited for a very specific type of reporting:

- *The vertical bar graph* is most useful for visual summaries of related financial information over a period of time.
- *The horizontal bar graph* should be used to compare two or more related results at one moment or over a limited time period.
- *The line graph* should report the progress of one type of information (such as sales, orders, or costs) or of two related facts (such as current versus previous year's sales, actual compared with forecast, or sales compared with direct costs).
- *The circle graph* is the most limited form. It is appropriate only for reporting breakdowns of a well-understood single unit. For example, a circle graph can show how the average dollar of revenue is spent during the year.

Using a combination of graphs in reports can add variety, especially when a large number of visual aids are called for. However, similarly reported information should be restricted to the same graph form, and at the same size and scale.

Vertical Bar Graphs

Figure 6-1 shows a vertical bar graph. The vertical lines represent value in this case, while the horizontal scale is for either time or comparison. A vertical graph is so-called because value is always shown from top to bottom. Most people are accustomed to seeing this format, so you will probably use the vertical bar graph most.

The level of office supplies, revenues, or any other financial information over a period of time can be shown using a vertical bar graph. This graph is also useful for showing more than one factor. A bar can be broken into different sections (for example, a separate section for each division's contribution to a company's revenues) and the series of bars would reflect the changing condition of each section as well as the overall rise and fall of the bars as a whole. The problem with reporting multiple factors is that trends can be lost. If your graphs are too complex, the reader will get no more sense of significance than if no graphs were included at all.

Figure 6-1.   Vertical bar graph.

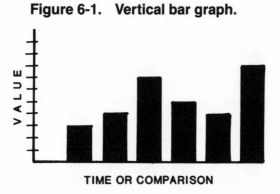

TIME OR COMPARISON

For example, one company reports revenues for several divisions, and includes a vertical bar graph that combines the information. With four divisions, it is difficult to see singular increases and decreases and to see easily whether overall trends are positive or negative.

One solution is to limit the scope of graphs. By preparing one per division, for example, and then summarizing the report with a consolidated graph, the information is much clearer for the reader. Limit what you report on a graph according to the following rule: Report one or two factors over a period of time (demonstrating a trend) or report multiple factors for one period only (to compare different results). For example, a company reporting revenues for several divisions could use the vertical bar graph to show a single division's sales over a period of time. It could also compare the different divisions during the current quarter only.

Horizontal Bar Graphs

A horizontal bar graph like the one shown in Figure 6-2 is appropriate for combining several related information summaries. In all graphic reporting, time should be displayed as progressing from the left to the right side of the graph. So the horizontal graph is less applicable for progressive information. Use this as a summary of value for a particular time (such as the current month or quarter); and use the individual bars to represent different factors at the particular time. You can break a horizontal bar into several parts by encoding the bar itself. For example, in Figure 6-3 five separate divisions' revenues are reported on a single horizontal bar graph, and a legend of the codes is included underneath.

Line Graphs

The line graph is also useful for comparing information visually. It has a wide number of applications, such as comparisons of actual with projected results, sales and net profits, and the performances of different divisions or departments. The line graph can be used to measure performance in a statistical process control system, to track defects, and to spot trends. In Figure 6-4, an actual versus projected line graph shows a definite trend over a period of time.

Figure 6-2.   Horizontal bar graph.

Circle Graphs

The last type—the circle graph—should be used sparingly and only for certain types of reports. Since the entire circle represents 100 percent, only some forms of information will be appropriate. For example, the changing distribution of sales by division over time can be significant but almost impossible to show on a circle graph. Changes over time are made most visual on a bar or line graph. A circle, though, can do only one thing: break down the condition of 100 percent (the full circle) into a number of slices. And it can do this only as of a single moment.

The circle graph does not clearly show a trend, as vertical bar graphs can do. A series of circle graphs, showing emerging changes over time,

Figure 6-3.   Comparative reporting.

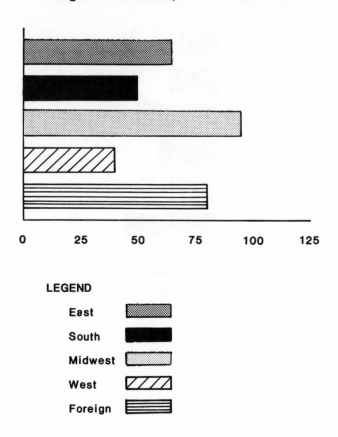

can be used in a report. However, they will not highlight the significance of those changes as clearly as if the same information is placed on a bar graph.

One thing you can do well on a circle graph is to show where each dollar of revenue goes. For example, you can include slices of the circle that represent salaries, advertising, and other major expenses. Net profits

Figure 6-4.   Line graph.

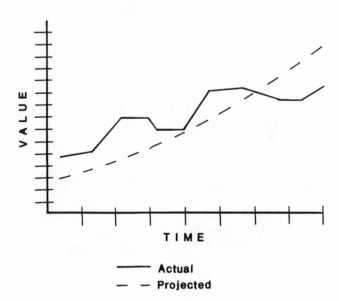

can be highlighted by shading a portion of the circle graph. This technique is shown in Figure 6-5.

Scale should be precise when preparing a circle graph. This requires conversion from percentages to degrees. For example, you want to break a circle into the following portions:

Salaries and Wages	46%
Rent	12
Advertising	21
Other Expenses	18
Net Profit	3
Total	100%

Figure 6-5.   Circle graph.

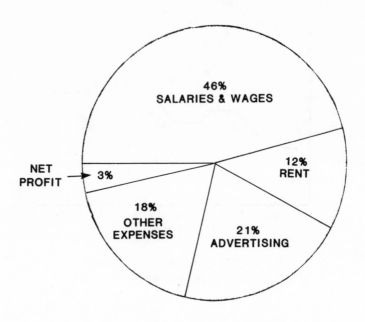

To calculate exactly how the circle of 360 degrees should be broken up, you need a protractor. Multiply each percentage by 360 and round off to the closest degree:

$$
\begin{array}{rcrcr}
46\% & \times & 360 & = & 166 \\
12 & \times & 360 & = & 43 \\
21 & \times & 360 & = & 75 \\
18 & \times & 360 & = & 65 \\
3 & \times & 360 & = & \underline{11} \\
 & \text{Total} & & & 360
\end{array}
$$

Next, draw a base line representing zero degrees from the center of the circle to the outside. Using this base, find the calculated degree with the

Figure 6-6.   Converting degrees.

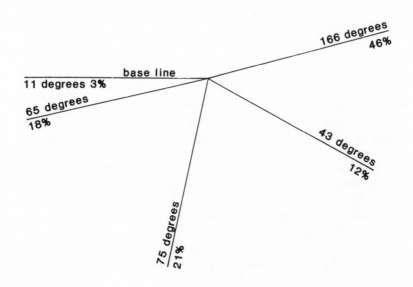

protractor and draw lines from the center to those points. Each line you draw becomes a new base line for calculating the next segment, until you have gone full circle. This makes the segments of your circle representative of the percentage you need. This technique is shown in Figure 6–6.

EXPLAINING YOUR GRAPH

Never place a graph in a report and expect the reader to understand precisely what you mean without extra information. You can provide this support in several ways:

- Text explanations
- Titles
- Captions
- In-graph wording
- Annotations
- Footnotes
- Coded legends

Graphs should be discussed in your narrative section, so they are a part of your report that the reader both needs and uses. The purpose of including graphs is not to add outside information, but to make the report easier to understand.

The title of a graph should be simple, yet clear. Be sure the title tells exactly what the graph is summarizing. For example, if you prepare a vertical line chart showing an *increase* in the percentage of net profits, don't call the graph "Net Profits Over Six Months." Call it "Percentage Increase in Net Profits Over Six Months."

Captions can be useful when a graph might otherwise not be as clear as you'd like. Using the example of a percentage increase, you can use captions under the graph. For example:

The graph shows a trend in the growth of net profits over the previous six months. Each bar represents a percentage increase or decrease in comparison to the previous month.

Use in-graph text sparingly. You do not want to clutter your graph with distracting and unneeded words and phrases. Consider replacing a coded legend when a short description will work better. For example, you prepare a line graph showing revenues in comparison with your forecast. Label a solid line with the single word "Actual" and a broken line with "Projected" and explain outside the graph what revenues you are talking about.

Annotation, like in-graph text, should be used only when that's the best possible way to add an explanation. If you find there's a need for excessive annotation, your graph is not clear or simple enough. Annotation can be used to show exceptions. For example, you are reporting on inventory levels. During the year, you brought in goods previously stored in another location, which causes a sudden jump in inventory levels. You can annotate this by drawing a line from the increase and explaining, "Includes 9,200 parts added from other location."

Footnotes can be useful instead of annotation or captions when there is a need for more explanation than ususal. For example, you are preparing a graph showing the number of customer calls each month. You might use footnotes to explain unusual changes in the level of calls. Place a letter by the change, draw a circle around the letter, and include your explanation below the graph, preceded by the letter corresponding to your in-graph reference.

Coded legends enable you to report several different factors in one graph (particularly in bar graph form), without excessive use of words. But overuse of legends can make the graph unattractive or confusing. Be sure to include a legend explaining the meaning of shadings, colored in area, or other codes you use.

Avoid using in-graph text, annotation, and footnotes except in the rarest of circumstances. It's much better to let a graph stand with little beyond the title and a brief caption, and explain what it shows in the narrative section of your report.

KEEPING GRAPHICS IN PERSPECTIVE

Your graphs and charts should be simple and to the point. The truly successful visual aid is the one that speaks volumes but is clear and uncluttered. Graphics add life to a report. They also can ruin it if you use them too heavily. Follow these guidelines:

1. Be certain that you need a graphic representation to present information clearly.
2. Limit the number of graphs you include to achieve a reasonable balance with the narrative.
3. Keep it simple. Don't make your graphs so complex that they're difficult to interpret.
4. Don't vary the types of graphs you use when reporting similar information. If reporting a series of related trends, report them on the same type of graph and to the same scale.
5. Tie graphs to narrative sections. A report that includes a section

of graphs by itself won't be as effective as one that interrelates the graphs with the text. Be sure the narrative section refers to a graph and place the graph on the same page as your discussion, or on the page immediately before or after.

6. Don't repeat information. If you have summarized financial information on a graph, you don't have to go into a lot of detail in your narrative. You can refer to significant changes in a trend or compare facts to a previous period, but let the graph speak for itself.

Graphs cannot stand alone. You need narratives, not only to explain important information on a graph, but to tell what the information means to the reader. You want your reports to be interpretative and—most of all—to draw conclusions and make specific recommendations. The same rules apply to graphic communications as apply to the narrative form. You must present facts in priority form, enable the reader to grasp a lot of information quickly, and make a statement that solves the problem.

In one report, a negative trend in expense variations was shown on a line graph. The actual and budgeted expenses were compared over a period of six months. By itself, that is very useful information and lets the reader visualize the problem. But that's only the start.

The graph is not a substitute for a good, informative report. It's only one mode of expression. As a tool for making your report interesting, a graph can be used to support the argument you want to make. For example, you make a recommendation in your report for revised internal controls. That argument is stronger when you show that there is a problem that your suggestion will correct. A graphic representation can point out a problem, just as it can highlight good news. But it isn't conclusive. It just sets the stage and makes your report more convincing.

WORK PROJECT

1. You want to summarize a report on revenues by including a graph. You must show the information for the previous four quarters and explain revenue trends in four divisions. What type of graph should you use, how many different graphs should be prepared, and why?

2. A graph is entitled "Office Supply Expenses, One Year," and shows the percentage increase each month in comparison with the previous month. What's wrong with this title, and how would you change it? In addition, what would you say in a caption to clarify what the graph shows?

3. Of total advertising expenses last year, 38 percent was spent on newspaper ads, 24 percent on radio, 16 percent in direct mail, 17 percent in magazines, and 5 percent in other media. You want to show this breakdown on a circle graph. How many degrees will each expense represent?

7

Creative Reporting Forms

"There is no permanent, absolute, unchangeable truth; what we should pursue is the most convenient arrangement of our ideas."

—Samuel Butler

Sid prepared a report that clearly explained a very complex series of tasks. It included diagrams, cross-references, and graphics. His supervisor complimented him on the job. "I read your report and thought it was very creative," he said. "Thanks," Sid answered. "I thought so too. I even autographed it in the lower right-hand corner."

You probably won't be acknowledged as a gifted artist because of the quality of your reports. But you can produce reports that show some imagination and creativity. As long as the purpose of an unusual format is to improve reader comprehension, and as long as the report clarifies your message, you are not limited to traditional forms.

For example, you are preparing an especially complicated report. It contains seven sections and each section must be cross-referenced to another. Rather than trying to lead the reader through a complex maze, you combine narratives with graphics and show where the reader can

look for more information, if needed. One section summarizes and
refers the reader to another section or page, where detailed narratives,
financial information, and graphics are included. This is appropriate, for
example, when you give a profit and loss summary providing detailed
breakdowns in a later section.

MAKING REPORTS MORE READABLE

One example of creative reporting is the simple combination of narratives and graphics. In one company, a monthly report summarizes a
number of ratios for financial trends. The report has always consisted of
explanatory narratives, with ratios summarized in the back of the report.
The reader has to flip back and forth between sections—assuming he or
she is willing to make the effort to follow the report. A new manager
takes over the job and decides to revise the format, combining narratives
with graphics. Under the old format, one section of the report would
read:

> This month's current assets were $423,900, while liabilities
> were $199,100. The current ratio is 2.1 to 1, compared with a 2.0
> ratio during each of the past two months. Deducting inventories of
> $18,400 from assets, the company's quick assets ratio is 2.0 to 1,
> compared with a ratio of 1.9 last month and 1.7 the month before.
>   These ratios reflect a continuing improvement in working
> capital over the past year. We should expect a four-month decline
> in both current and quick assets ratios during the winter months,
> based on trends established during the past two years.

The reader must read through two paragraphs to get the essential
information. Also note that the conclusion and interpretation of the
significance in these results comes after the presentation of information.
The manager's new format, shown below, isolates the financial summaries and devotes the text to interpreting the facts, so the reader can get a
lot more information in about the same amount of space. For example:

The positive trend in working capital is continuing. Both current and quick assets ratios show continuing strength over the prior month and last year. The current ratio's level shows an improvement over the same ratio last year, when

Current Ratio

$$\frac{\$423,900}{\$199,100} = 2.1 \text{ to } 1$$

seasonal factors caused a 1.5 to 1 comparison. We expect no less than 2.0 to 1 in the future, given our increased financial strength.

Quick Assets Ratio

$$\frac{\$405,500}{\$199,100} = 2.0 \text{ to } 1$$

Assets continue to exceed liabilities by no less than a two-to-one margin. We should expect a four-month seasonal decline in both ratios, based on trends established during the past two years. The quick assets comparison is of limited significance, considering our growing dependency on inventories in stock. However, we suggest continuing the analysis for the purpose of comparing year-to-year trends.

In this instance, a brief summary of the numbers is set aside in the paragraph, so that the reader sees highlights of what is being discussed. Now, rather than using text to explain the ratio, the manager allows the numbers to speak for themselves. The space can be used to comment upon the significance of those numbers and to explain what should be expected in the near future.

FINANCIAL SUMMARIES IN TEXT

There are three traditional, but not always effective, ways to report financial information. They are:

1. Including an attached financial statement or summary, which consists of columns of numbers.
2. Breaking the text with charts.
3. Converting the financial information into narrative form.

In the first case, the reader has to turn to another page, where he or she is confronted with a list of purely numerical information. When you separate the narrative discussion from the financial summary, a lot of potential information will be lost. This format, which is the most common, is far from satisfactory. It doesn't encourage the reader to comprehend the information, and there is a tendency to include little in the way of comment. Typically, a report will simply read, "The quarter's production is shown on the attached summary."

That's a passive way to report. It's left to the reader to look for the significance in the report, and even if you attempt to tell the reader what the numbers mean and what to look for, the reader still has to refer back and forth between pages.

In the second format, adding a chart between paragraphs, the discussion is broken up. Again, there's a tendency to report passively by simply pointing out the chart's location: "Production is summarized in the chart below." This is an improvement over the first format only because the information is on the same page. But it still doesn't enable the reader to comprehend or interpret information *while* reading an explanation.

The third format is the least desirable of all. When you attempt to summarize financial information in a narrative form, you only make the information less clear. For example, you report on total revenues for the current quarter for four separate divisions. A purely narrative explanation might read:

> Revenues for the quarter, by division, were $193,500 in the East; $164,000 in the South; $123,400 in the Midwest; and $110,900 in the West. The total of $591,800 is a 2.3% increase over the same quarter last year, with increases occurring in the East and South and decreases in Midwest and Pacific divisions.
>
> Revenues rose by 6.9% in the East and by 7.3% in the South. Revenues fell by 1.5% in the Midwest and by 7.1% in the West.
>
> Revenues have been growing in the East and South divisions over the past two years, with a corresponding drop in revenues in the other two divisions.

This is a confusing format. The reader will either read it without comprehending the significance in the information or will have to put together a chart from what is reported. The most important point of the report—that there is a continuing negative trend—is left until the end. The reader has to get through a long, uninteresting explanation of the numbers before finding out what it all means.

There is a way to report this information without using any of the three traditional formats. If you incorporate and summarize the key factors in text, you will clarify and highlight the report. This allows you to spend narrative space interpreting the information, while the reader can see at a glance what's going on in the different divisions.

Figure 7-1 shows how this report could be done. Notice that the narrative is now devoted to discussion and interpretation. No space is required for explaining the numbers, which the reader can see at a glance. This format clarifies the information and carries the reader through with an analysis. There's no need to go back and forth from a separate chart, or to plow through numbers within a paragraph.

GRAPHS IN TEXT

Incorporating a chart in a series of narrative discussions is certainly an improvement over all of the traditional methods of reporting. But giving financial information in chart form may still not completely communicate its significance. When a trend can be more clearly seen with a graphic representation, it would be better to report it in graphic form.

In the preceding example, a small increase in quarterly revenues consists of increases in two divisions that were offset by decreases in two others. It's also reported that this is part of a trend and not just an isolated factor this quarter. The financial information in this instance could be shown in a graph that would be much clearer for the reader.

Taking the example a step farther, what if you also wanted to show the relative share of net profits for each division, both this period and compared with the same period last year? This could be summarized with a graph and included in text.

Figure 7-2 shows how the same report could be prepared with the use of small graphs. These can be placed into paragraphs and referred to in text. When the numbers are taken out completely and replaced with graphs, it may also be necessary to attach a chart summarizing the

Figure 7-1.   Financial summaries in text.

Revenues in the four divisions of the company show a continuing trend as established
over the past two
years. While

REVENUES	
East	$193,500
South	164,000
Midwest	123,400
West	110,900
	$591,800

East and South
divisions report
continued growth
in volume each
quarter, those
gains are offset
by declines in both Midwest and West divisions.

The increase or decrease in sales by
division overall
was only 2.3%.

COMPARISON PRIOR YEAR	
East	+ 6.9%
South	+ 7.3
Midwest	− 1.5
West	− 7.1
	+ 2.3%

It should be
noted that sub-
stantial gains
in the East and
South were di-
luted by declines
in other divisions, notably in the West.

Figure 7-2.   Graphs in text.

The mix of revenues among the company's
four divisions reflects a continuing trend.
While revenues are on the
rise in the East and South
divisions, they are on a
decline in the Midwest and
West. This trend has been
followed over the past
two years, and shows a
distinct pattern that
has not varied due to seasonal factors.

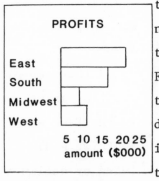

There is a direct relationship between
the trend in gross reve-
nues and the trend in
the mix of net profits.
For the current quar-
ter, East and South
divisions report growth
in both revenues and
their share of overall
net profits for the company. The other two
divisions report a corresponding decline.

information in dollars and cents. This satisfies the reader who wants to have the actual amounts, without sacrificing the clarity and simplicity the graphs add to your report.

The previous examples showed how to report financial information in either chart or graph form with narrative explanations. You can also express this using a combined chart and graph without the need for narratives. Figure 7-3 shows how this can be accomplished.

A chart shows the overall summary of total revenues, expenses, and net profits. The charts compare the same information by division for both the current and previous years. This saves a great deal of time and space. On one page, you are showing:

1. Revenues
   - For the entire organization
   - By division
   - Compared with the previous year
2. Net profits
   - For the entire organization
   - By division
   - Compared with the previous year

This one page eliminates the need for a great deal of narrative explanation. Whenever you find yourself devoting a lot of space telling the reader what the results are, you should consider replacing that text with a chart, graph, or a combination of the three elements. Then your narrative can very quickly point out any significant trends, rather than telling what should be shown.

Set a reporting standard when dealing with numerical information (including any form of reporting that involves quantities, whether of employees, customers, production, or dollars), such as limiting yourself to one page of comment. If you need more than that, you can probably say it better without words.

Use that one page to tell the reader what the numbers mean, not in terms of the numbers themselves, but as an interpretation. In the example above, you might take one page to make observations about the reported results. Why is it that revenues and profits are up over the previous year in East and South divisions and down in the West and Midwest?

Figure 7-3. Graphic summary of financial information.

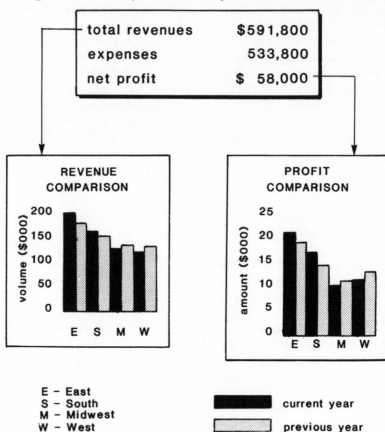

Some questions might include:

1. Is there a problem of managing the more remote locations?
2. Is the competition stronger in some regions?
3. Have the Midwest and West divisions been in operation fewer years?
4. Are sales representatives not trained as well in some regions?

Your report is much more valuable if the narrative is devoted to examination and interpretation than if it simply reports the numbers. Do not expect readers to interpret information on their own. Your job in a report is to present facts and interpret them so that the reader knows what those facts mean. You should use current and past information to show the reader how a negative trend must be corrected or how a positive trend must be encouraged. You're not just reporting what has occurred. Your report is valuable only when it goes beyond the facts and figures.

WORK PROJECT

1. In a report on general expense variances from the company's budget, you develop the following facts in one account:

Month	Budget	Actual	Variance
Jan	$ 3,000	$ 3,450	$(450)
Feb	3,000	3,235	(235)
Mar	3,200	3,610	(410)
Apr	3,200	3,714	(514)
May	2,900	3,519	(619)
Jun	2,900	3,601	(701)
Total	$18,200	$21,129	$(2,929)

How can the significance of this information be best summarized in your report, and what comments should accompany it?

2. You prepare a report each month that presents a series of financial ratios and explains how the trends compare with previous

periods. This has been a strictly narrative report in the past. How can the ratios be more clearly highlighted in your report?

3. A summary of the progress on a number of projects under contract in your company includes charts for each job showing the original plan and current progress toward a deadline. Each job has its own section, so that the reader cannot review the status of all jobs in one place. How can you consolidate the report, make it clearer, and highlight the important information the reader needs?

8
Reporting Work Flow

> *"All echelons of the staff will coordinate the configuration of the plans with the requisite tailoring of the overview in order to expedite the functional objective."*
>
> —Capt. Scarett Adams, USN

The bakery manager in a fortune cookie factory suggested to the vice president that production work-flow procedures be improved. The vice president responded, "The procedures have been tested and reviewed and are to be followed to the letter." The manager shrugged and answered, "As you say. But it would be a lot easier to put the fortune into the cookies before folding them up."

Whether you're stuffing fortunes into cookies, controlling a project's schedule, or keeping expenses within a budget, you probably follow an accepted procedure. But nothing remains the same for long in an expanding company. Procedures must change with changing demand and should be modified continuously.

Written procedures help in training new employees and in ensuring that controls are followed and deadlines met. In addition, writing down what you and your employees do is the best way to test a procedure and its validity. It is often true that through testing you will discover more efficient ways to complete a task.

Explaining what you do in writing is one of those jobs that no one seems to have the time to do. And when the time is available, we find this job to be one of the least enjoyable. For the manager trying to get employees to document their jobs, it might take more than a single request, and it is likely that the first attempt will prove inadequate.

Task descriptions are step-by-step explanations of how to do a job. They should include the sequence of steps, deadlines, location and use of materials (such as reports, information from other departments, or forms), and examples of final work. The useful task description will also explain where information comes from and where it goes when the responsible person is done with it.

Why should employees write down this information? Simply, to make sure that every job can be done by someone else. However, people have an aversion to putting down on paper exactly what they do, and this fear is understandable. While we might not admit it, the fear is that explaining our jobs makes us replaceable.

This is a problem for every manager. You should insist on having updated, usable task descriptions from everyone in your department, but you must also convince them that the purpose is not to replace them. In one insurance company, a manager was able to get her administrative assistant to write a task description only by making this point: In the event of promotion opportunities, you're more likely to be moved up if someone else can be put into your job easily. That requires a task description that anyone can use. If you are the only person who knows how to do your job, the company can't afford to promote you.

That same company had experienced great difficulties in the previous year, when a large number of employees had left. With unusually high turnover, a number of new managers and supervisors did not know how their employees did certain tasks, and in some cases, there was no one left in a department who had done the tasks more than once or twice before.

GOING FOR SIMPLICITY

Nothing is too complex to explain in simple terms. It's just a matter of breaking a description down into steps, making sure nothing has been left out, and explaining it thoroughly.

Instruct employees to keep the reader in mind when explaining work flow. It should always be assumed that the reader is completely unfamiliar with the procedures the employee follows. To reduce the employee's possible fear of writing down the details of a job and to help him or her give you what you want, tell why the task description is needed. It can be required for one of several reasons:

- *For a procedures manual.* When a company puts together a complete procedures manual, individual tasks are of less significance than major responsibilities of a job. At this level, the work flow procedure should be brief and concise.
- *For a manager.* When you ask for a task description for your own use, the employee is most likely to resist, thinking the request is the step just before termination or some other change. Explain exactly why you need it. Are you putting together a department procedures manual, or are you only concerned with job coverage in case of vacation or sick time? At this level, all details of the task should be included: materials used, forms and reports (with filled-in samples), deadlines, sources of information, and where the final product of the task goes.
- *For conversions.* You might also need work-flow descriptions from employees as part of a conversion from one system to another. For example, when functions are taken from manual to automated processing, it's necessary to identify the volume of transactions, specifics of input and output, and the need for file storage.

In all of these examples, the key is keeping it simple. Show employees how to write brief narrative descriptions. They should use the outline form as much as possible, which is easiest for someone unfamiliar with the task to follow. They should always attach samples of all worksheets, forms, reports, and other documents involved in the procedure.

Example: One department manager asks an employee to write a summary of the process for approving check requests generated from within the department. The employee writes this first draft:

Check requests are submitted by employees with information filled in: date, name of the payee, address, brief description of the

> payment, payment date, coding, and amount. I check the coding
> and compare the amount to the invoice or receipt attached to the
> check request. No payments can be made without documentation.
> If all is in order, I sign the request and forward it to the vice
> president for review and a second signature.

That's a fairly clear description of the procedure, but someone unfamiliar
with it might have trouble following the sequence. The manager asks for
another version in outline form. The second draft reads:

Procedure:	Approval of check requests.
Source:	Departmental employees submit completed check request forms (sample attached) and invoices or other documentation.
Form:	The following information must be filled in on the check request form before the procedure can continue:

- Date
- Payee name and address
- Description of payment
- Payment date
- Coding

Steps:	The manager of the department follows these steps:

1. Compare requested amount to invoice—verify.
2. Check coding—verify or correct.
3. If there is a coding error, instruct employee for future check requests.
4. Sign form on "approval" line.
5. Forward to vice president for review and second signature.

From this revised work-flow description, anyone unfamiliar with the
procedure can use it without any problem. Note that a sample form is
attached to the description. This is extremely helpful, because the reader
has the actual form to refer to.

THE VERTICAL FLOWCHART

Another tool that clarifies a procedure is the vertical flowchart. The value in this tool is that it makes the procedure visual, so that the reader can review the steps in a procedure, identify points where decisions must be made, and see the entire process from beginning to end.

Using the same example as in the previous section, the procedure for approving check requests starts when employees submit the requests and attached invoices and ends when the approved requests are forwarded for a second approval. All of the steps in between can be reduced to a visual form. This is a relatively short procedure and serves well for example. This technique is especially useful, though, for more involved functions. The flowchart shown in Figure 8-1 is an example of how a visual summary can be done.

Writing up your procedure this way also helps you to check your own work. If you do the same thing day after day, it's easy to leave out important steps. But by putting it down in flowchart form, you force yourself to include every step.

Employees who have well organized, step-by-step procedures are better able to check their own work and to ensure that all tasks are completed on time with a minimum of errors. You should emphasize the importance of quality and consistency when requesting task-flow descriptions. Flowcharts are effective because they force people to follow the correct procedural steps.

Most useful to the reader who is unfamiliar with the job are the decision points: places where the flow can go one way or the other. These are the most important parts of a work flow analysis, but they are left out of many purely narrative descriptions.

Keeping flowcharts simple and uncomplicated is desirable. Someone who sees a flowchart for the first time is likely to become discouraged, especially if the accompanying narrative is difficult to follow or incomplete. But when an especially complex flowchart must be built, you might want to use differently shaped boxes for processes, decision points, and page-to-page references. Templates for flowcharts contain 10 or more different shapes. Keep your design as simple as possible, but remember that varied shapes can clarify the meaning of each box. Typical flowchart symbols are shown in Figure 8-2.

(text continues on page 90)

Figure 8-1.   Vertical flowchart.

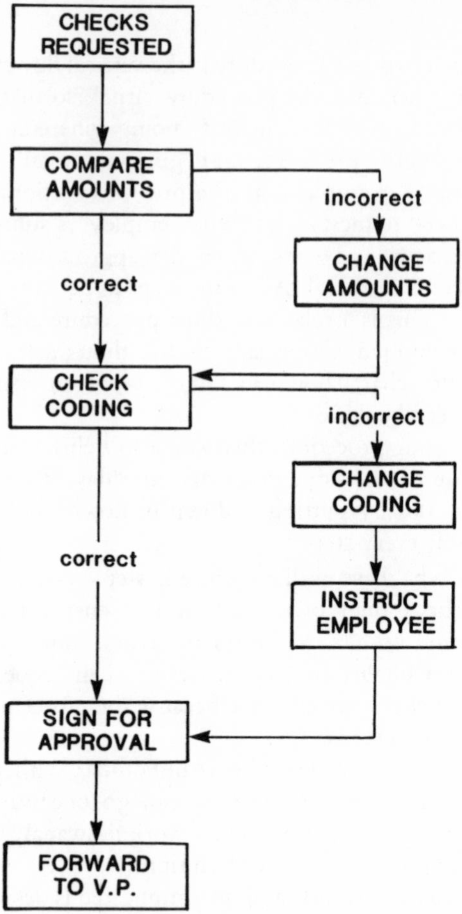

Figure 8-2.   Flowchart symbols.

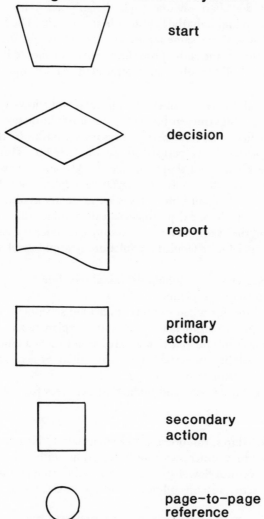

start

decision

report

primary
action

secondary
action

page-to-page
reference

The easiest work-flow summaries to review are those that combine narrative and flowchart on one page. It isn't necessary to draw the flowchart, just to highlight the key steps in the margin. The full flowchart can be included with the same report to serve as a review of steps once a reader comprehends the entire procedure. This idea should be used when a process is especially involved or complicated. An example is shown in Figure 8-3.

The vertical flowchart can clarify a process and allows you to report work flow in a straightforward manner. But it has limitations. It is most appropriate when only one person performs a task. In the example shown, the procedure is performed by one person. That individual maintains the record and draws up the weekly and monthly reports, depending on outsiders only for narrative explanations for behind-schedule projects. In reality, most tasks are more involved. Many people play a part, not just in one department but throughout the organization.

To expand the example, if the procedure explained the entire process of tracking actual and scheduled completion, it would involve:

1. Procedures for developing the initial schedule
2. Approval of completion deadlines
3. Procedures for when projects fall behind schedule
4. Appropriate commentary in narrative explanations
5. Responsibility for tracking and reaction to scheduling problems
6. Responsibility for establishing the initial project schedule and advance planning of staff time
7. Forecasting income and budgeting expenses for individual projects

Like most procedures, this doesn't occur in isolation. No one department or individual does much without interaction with others. In these instances, the vertical flowchart can become confusing and unclear. You can't identify actual responsibilities, priorities, or deadlines.

THE HORIZONTAL FLOWCHART

The vertical flowchart is appropriate for limited descriptions. But for a more expanded and comprehensive report, consider reporting on a horizontal flowchart.

Figure 8-3.   Flowchart combined with text.

Tracking Project Completion

This is a procedure for tracking actual completion of projects compared against the scheduled completion time. The purpose is to ensure that projects are kept on schedule.

The procedure begins when a project is first initiated. The first step is to summarize the schedule on a chart format.

Project Initiated
▼
Schedule Charted
▼

Although reporting occurs monthly, tracking entries are made to the schedule every week. On Friday afternoon ("Thursday" if Friday is a holiday), the portion of a project completed to date is entered on the job schedule.

Weekly Entries
▼

If the completion is behind schedule, a project report is prepared immediately and submitted to the department's manager. Otherwise, no report is prepared until month-end.

Behind Schedule?
▼   ▼
yes   no ──┐
▼   │
Project Report │
▼   │
Monthly Report ◄┘
▼

At month-end, all project status is summarized on the Monthly Project Report form. Narrative explanations for all behind-schedule projects are collected from project managers and attached to the report. The report is submitted to the department manager no later than the fifth working day of the new month.

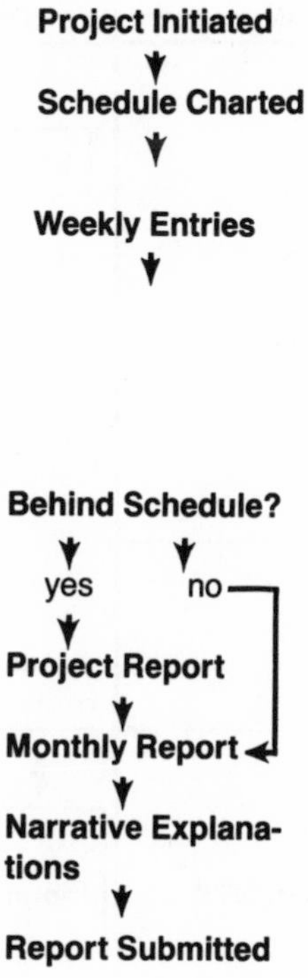

Narrative Explanations
▼
Report Submitted

This reporting format clarifies multi–person or multi–departmental work. The left–to–right part of the flowchart is a summary of process and time, and the top–to–bottom is an identification of documents and responsibility. This format is summarized in Figure 8-4.

Each person or department is given a single line detailing its

Figure 8-4.   Horizontal flowchart.

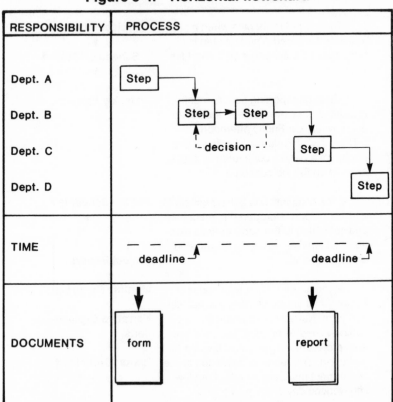

responsibilities. Everything that is to be performed by that person appears on the line and is listed in chronological order. Whenever a decision must be made, a loop is drawn, one line for a "yes" answer and the other for a "no" answer. For example, in describing the procedure for tracking projects, the decision step asks, "Is the report behind schedule?" If the answer is no, the individual proceeds to the next step. If the answer is yes, then a weekly report must be drawn up and submitted.

Time is another factor that should be reported on a flowchart. But on the more limited vertical form, this is not possible. On the horizontal flowchart, a single line for time is included below the responsibility section. All deadlines are written in at the appropriate point on this line. For example, in the project-tracking procedure, entries to the schedules are made each Friday, and any needed weekly reports are done the same day or on the following Monday. At the end of the month, a monthly status report is completed by the fifth working day of the new month. The "time" line reports these deadlines:

Steps	Make weekly entries	Prepare weekly report	Prepare monthly report
Time	Friday	Monday	5th working day

Finally, any documents involved in the procedure are described at the point in the process that they are to be prepared. Using the same example as above, the horizontal flowchart should look like this:

Steps	Make weekly entries	Prepare weekly report	Prepare monthly report
Time	Friday	Monday	5th working day
Documents		Weekly report	Monthly report

The horizontal flowchart includes all of the elements for a complete description. The responsibility is listed by person or department, so that the steps in the process are identified as they proceed from one person to another in the company. The deadlines are listed and all documents are described at the appropriate point in the process.

All of this ties in nicely with narratives that also describe the procedure. In many instances, you will ask employees to provide outlines and other narrative descriptions with their flowcharts, perhaps in great detail. The horizontal flowchart enables you to build a fully documented procedure with complete descriptions *and* cross-referencing features. The accompanying report should include filled-in forms and reports, for example. A new employee can use these for reference, and also will be able to see where they fit in the procedure, when they're due, and how to interact with other departments.

The horizontal flowchart proves the validity of work flow or points out flaws in controls and processes. For example, a weak link in a procedure will become evident as you try to reduce it to a horizontal flowchart. The identification of flaws and weak links is apparent in the following ways:

- Whenever there is a need to show two or more steps occurring at the same time, the procedure is weakened. For the procedure to continue, two or more people must perform separate functions. If either one fails, deadlines may be missed and the entire procedure must stop.
- Every time the steps proceed from one department to another, there's an opportunity for miscommunication or other breakdowns. In every procedure, the exchange of work and processes from one location to another should be viewed as a control point where problems are likely to occur.
- When several departments contribute to a procedure immediately before a deadline, that's another danger point. Consider ways to revise procedures to avoid depending upon several different sources at that time. In some cases, steps may be executed well in advance of deadline.

In the example of check-approval procedures, there are three responsibilities involved: the employee who submits the check request, the manager who checks and approves it, and the vice president who receives the final, approved forms. In the first step, the employee submits a filled-in check request (a form should be indicated at the bottom of the flowchart). From that point forward, the manager is responsible for most of the steps and will involve the employee only if coding errors are discovered. The last step is submitting the day's check requests to the vice president. This requires a time indicator (daily) and a document note (the check requests).

Horizontal flowcharts can become quite long and involved when a procedure is complicated. For example, the entire process of paying bills will involve several departments, from requisitioning through general ledger and budget reporting. To keep the reports simple, break up a long procedure into natural, smaller units. The manager's job starts with the submission of a check request and ends when the daily forms are sent on. That can be made into one work-flow report.

If your report must involve all other phases before and after that one, identify the different parts of the whole in the report, and be sure that each one begins where the last one left off. You must be careful that no steps are left out in the overall summary of a larger job.

DEFINING RESPONSIBILITY

Besides describing functions and paperwork, your work-flow report should discuss responsibility. The vertical flowchart is not designed for this. The horizontal method shows it at a glance. When several departments are involved in a procedure, be prepared to include a section in your report that discusses this issue.

A responsibility within a procedure is not always limited to one isolated section of work flow. For example, an employee prepares a check request and, at first glance, that appears to be the end of the employee's role in the function. But there's more responsibility involved, such as filling out the form correctly and making the right coding decisions. There may be more to do later in the procedure, too.

The narrative section of your report dealing with responsibility should discuss the overall range of duties. One employee or department may be involved at several steps in the procedure *and* have a general responsibility for ensuring the work flow itself. Even a detailed flowchart cannot always show this, and the reader may need to understand the range of duties each person or department represents.

A complete report on work flow should include these sections:

1. Overview and explanation
   - Contents of the report
   - Purpose of the report
   - Identification of phases
2. Areas of responsibility
   - Individuals or departments
   - Responsibility for processes
3. Phase identification
   - Phases of the procedure
   - Relationship between phases
4. Documents
   - Forms and reports
   - Blank or filled-in samples
5. Flowcharts

Reporting work flow is often viewed as tedious and even unnecessary. Every time a change occurs, the procedure must be revised. If that's given a low priority, existing procedures soon become obsolete and cannot be used for their intended purpose. You can make work-flow reporting valuable and interesting by striving for clarity in form. Ultimately, a well-described procedure is made easier, and you will be able to identify opportunities for improved efficiency.

WORK PROJECT

1. Part-time employees in your department are paid by the hour. Each employee fills out a time report and submits it to you for approval. These are forwarded to the payroll department each week. Write a brief description in outline form of the steps involved in completing, approving, and forwarding time reports.

2. Prepare a brief vertical flowchart of the time-report procedure outlined above, including decision points.

3. Show how the same procedure could be summarized on a horizontal flowchart, including responsibility, deadlines, and forms.

9

When Not to Write a Report

"I do not object to people looking at their watches when I am speaking. But I strongly object when they start shaking them to make sure they are still going."

—Lord Birkett

The president asked the office manager for a report on ideas for improving internal assignment procedures. The manager suggested reducing the number of committees, with the comment that giving individual assignments was more likely to get results. The president was pleased with the idea and said, "Let's appoint a few of our best people to study this idea and put it into effect."

When committees meet, a bureaucracy is created. You might discover that some of the reports being done today in your company were devised months or even years ago by a "collective mind," and that now no one really reads the report. If that is true, there's probably a reason: The report simply might not be needed.

What can you do about this situation? Over time, a number of time-consuming reports might be devised and then go out of date later. Yet, when you run up against the corporate mind-set, you will find that eliminating a report is much more difficult than creating one.

ELIMINATING A REPORT

Reducing the amount of work your department does each month will cut expenses and free up time for other, more important tasks.

Be aware of the tendency in business to add more work, but rarely to reduce tasks. A critical review of the reports you prepare each month could lead to obvious ways to reduce your work load, such as:

1. *Consolidation.* Some reports can be combined.
2. *Simplification.* Some reports' formats can be made simpler and easier to follow; the current level of detail may be too high.
3. *Variation.* Some reports can be prepared in very brief form, with periodic versions that have more detailed information.
4. *Elimination.* Some reports can be done away with altogether. In some cases, reports originally requested as one-time projects end up as recurring ones just out of habit.
5. *Reduced frequency.* Some reports done each month might be better prepared quarterly, semiannually, or annually.

Example: In one insurance company, two departments are consolidated under one manager. Upon reviewing the work load, she discovers that a number of monthly reports are being prepared, and she concludes that some are out of date and no longer needed. Others duplicate information or provide no real value for the readers.

In all, ten reports are questionable. They had been requested at some time in the past, and simply continue to be produced from one month to another. The manager has a problem, though. How can she stop producing the reports without authority?

She writes a memo to everyone on the distribution list, suggesting that certain reports should either be eliminated or consolidated. Others, she suggests, can be prepared quarterly rather than every month. She asks for opinions and suggestions. It becomes necessary to visit some people, because the memo is not answered by everyone on the list.

As a result of this, the manager is able to do away with three of the ten reports. Two others are still needed, but only quarterly. And two other reports are combined into one. The reduction in work load is substantial. The changes free up about 15 hours per month, meaning less overtime and less pressure on everyone in the department. Most of the people on the distribution list had been filing the monthly reports, never even looking at them.

You can eliminate unneeded reports in your department, although you should proceed with caution. You might assume that no one reads them when, in fact, someone depends on the information for actions or decisions that you are not even aware of. Be sure you eliminate a report only after determining that everyone concerned approves of the decision. You will always experience difficulty simply stopping a report, because other people will want to continue receiving it each month—even when they don't read the report.

Expect resistance if you suggest that a report be stopped. Any bureaucracy will resist a reduction in work, and some people will actually feel threatened by your idea. There are many symbols of power and influence in a company, including location of a department, the number of employees, *and* the amount of internal mail received. When you suggest to a manager that he or she should no longer get a copy of a monthly report, it could be interpreted as a threat, a reduction of power and influence in the organization.

No one will admit to thinking that way, and everyone will agree that the attitude is a poor one. Yet, as everyone working in a company knows, attitudes about esteem and influence are very real. Everyone claims to be in favor of cutting costs, making work valid, and contributing to profits. But in reality, some employees are more concerned with appearing powerful.

Even asking people if their name can be removed from a distribution list can be very threatening. They measure their importance in terms of being included on a distribution list. Cutting back on distribution might make sense and save time and money in photocopying, but removing a name from the list will be a delicate issue.

You should approach this problem with diplomacy. Send a memo to everyone on the list, stating that you are reviewing distribution. Ask whether they need to continue receiving the report. In this way, no one will feel threatened by the suggestion that they should no longer get a copy. They might respond by saying yes, they do need to get a copy, or they might answer that they never understood why they received it in the first place. The important point is that you cannot simply stop sending the report to someone because you don't think they need it. That is certain to create a negative response.

FIVE ALTERNATIVES TO REPORTS

Just as a valuable and concise report demonstrates your ability, it's often true that *not* doing a report can prove your value to the company. If you desire to reduce work without losing its benefits, you will be recognized as a valuable member of the organization. For example, one report takes a lot of time every month, and you are sure that its value is limited. But you are told it cannot be eliminated because several people want to continue receiving it. This is not the end of your options. There is still a chance that you can reduce work load and cut back on the scope of the task. There are five possible ways to achieve this:

Modifying Content

Is everything in the report really needed? Perhaps a shorter, summarized version will be just as acceptable to the people who receive it. You can save time and effort by asking permission to prepare a shorter version of the same report. Many one–time reports must include a detailed analysis of one issue and are necessarily comprehensive. But a recurring report, one that monitors a trend or updates status from one month to another, can often be shortened. Avoid the pitfall of believing that all reports have to be long. There's nothing wrong with a one-page summary when that is all that's required to resolve the important question the reader needs answered.

Example: A manager in a consulting firm prepares a monthly report, showing status of all ongoing jobs in relation to their original schedules. He suggests shortening the report by including only those projects that were running behind schedule. The idea was approved, and a 22-page report was cut to under 10 pages. The issue in this case was, "Are any projects behind schedule, and if so, why?" There was no need to include information about projects that had no problems.

Reducing Frequency

The report might be needed only at the end of each quarter instead of each month. Many recurring reports are automatically assumed to be needed every month. But an analysis of what the reader needs will often suggest that a less frequent preparation is sufficient. The savings can be considerable. For example, doing a report quarterly instead of monthly will cut two-thirds of the work load. If you can apply the savings to a large number of reports in several departments, that adds up to a lot over the course of a year. Always look for ways to cut down on tasks.

Example: An underwriting manager in an insurance company prepares a study of trends in types of policies sold. The study is used in the preparation of a quarterly financial report that is sent to the president, so the manager recommends doing the study at the end of each quarter. The first response is negative. The vice president, who prepares the quarterly financial report, says he needs the summary every month. But when the manager points out that the financial report is done only four times per year, the vice president realizes that he only refers to the latest summary. He approves the change.

Consolidating Similar Reports

Some reports duplicate other reports. This inefficiency is tolerated because internal communication is not always as effective as it should be. One department might prepare two or more very similar reports without even considering the inefficiency of it. The solution is up to you. Appraise your work load realistically, and strive to eliminate unncessary labor whenever possible.

Example: The accounting manager in a public relations company prepares three reports concerned with budgets that include similar information. He recommends one report, observing that each of the departments on the distribution list would still be able to extract what they need. To make his point, he prepares the report on the revised format he suggests. His idea is accepted, enabling him to eliminate several hours of work each month.

Replacing a Report

Some reports contain a lot of information, when the reader is interested in only a few points. It might be that when a report was first requested, many questions needed to be answered—but only in the first report. Now, months or years later, the report might include a few relevant bits of information and a lot of unnecessary sections repeated from month to month. The idea of replacing the report with a shorter, faster form of communication—like a memo—might not occur to you, because you know someone else needs the information. But always question the content. You will find that some reports can be replaced with a much shorter message.

Example: The manager of the data processing department in a securities firm prepares a monthly report that summarizes ongoing work and lists the time before new projects' deadlines and scheduled delivery dates for output. Much of the information is repeated from one month to the next. He sees that an internal memo could easily replace the report, with a more detailed explanation prepared twice per year.

Holding a Meeting

A report might be intended to solve a problem that could be more effectively handled in a face-to-face meeting. In large companies with many departments, the tendency to produce a large number of reports can actually reduce the level of communication. You already know how little contact you have with a department on another floor, for example. The reports you send back and forth might be unnecessary if you simply met once each month to address the underlying issues. The time required for the meeting might be much less than the time you're now spending in preparing and sending out a report—and the meeting would have better results.

Example: One manager is assigned to write a report about communication problems within the organization and is told to include recommendations to improve the situation. He suggests that a meeting of all managers would lead to a dialogue among several people, whereas a report would be done in isolation and would present only one point of view. In this case, the obvious solution hadn't occurred to anyone else and a report was not the answer.

QUESTIONING VALIDITY

Is a report valid? An existing report can be eliminated or the task reduced; but when a new report is proposed, it might not be necessary to prepare it at all.

When you apply the definition criteria—reader, reason, and content—you might find that a report is not really needed. In that case, you have a responsibility to argue against it. This is especially true when a report will be prepared periodically. A few years ago, a U.S. government study was conducted to determine what made people happy. The study took several months and cost more than $1 million. Among the conclusions were:

- Those in good health are happier than those who are not.
- People with steady incomes are happier than the unemployed.
- People who enjoy their jobs are happier than those who do not.

Huge bureaucracies are famous for spending money to find out the obvious. The study was conducted because the money was there, and opting to *not* conduct it was unthinkable. Unfortunately, the same mentality is often found in smaller companies on a more modest budget. If you are given the assignment of preparing a report that you're sure no one really needs, fight it. Insist on being given valid work, and resist spending your time and effort on tasks that make no sense.

The morale of employees in your department will be higher when they know the work they do has meaning. If the reports they prepare are filed away without being read, or if they contain a large volume of information that no one needs, the quality of all the work they do will suffer.

The manager who argues against doing unneeded work, who presents time-saving alternatives, and who questions assignments and offers better solutions is one who will be perceived positively. Not doing a report that shouldn't be done is just as impressive as doing a thorough job on a necessary report. Set the standard for yourself and your department that all of the work you do must have value and meaning. The tasks you perform cost the company money, so there should be a return on the investment in order to justify it.

WORK PROJECT

1. You prepare two reports in your department. One is sent to the manager of finance and contains dollar amounts; the other goes to the marketing director and shows percentage changes.

   a. How can you make the preparation of these similar reports more efficient?
   b. What procedure should you follow to get permission for the change you have in mind?

2. You report every month on the status of projects underway in your department. The purpose is to identify scheduling problems but, for most projects, you are not experiencing any difficulty. How can the size of the report be reduced without special permission?

3. One report goes to 14 different departments. You want to remove several names from the list to cut down on photocopying expenses. What is the danger in this idea, and how can you best achieve your objective?

10

Where to Go From Here

"Never forget that only dead fish swim with the stream."

—Malcolm Muggeridge

An employee turned in a 90-page report when the manager had expected a much shorter version. "Your reports don't have to be this long," she told the employee. "Keep it brief and forget about bulk. We're supposed to be providing information, not selling produce. Do you know how much it costs to write a 90-page report?" The employee answered, "Umm, do you mean, how much per pound?"

You are faced with a challenge. The employees in your department cannot be expected to understand how reports can be made valuable and will not set standards on their own. It's up to you to take the lead and train them in the techniques of written communication. Few people begin their reports by defining the reader, the reason, and the content. And few will question whether a report should continue to be produced. It takes a real effort to question the way things are being done. You have to set an example.

TAKING PRIDE IN WORK

Regardless of the type of report prepared in your department, set standards for content, accuracy, and appearance. For reports done in your department, insist that four rules always be followed:

1. *Make sure all information is accurate.* The easiest way to lose credibility in your organization is to issue a report with inaccuracies or outright errors of fact. Be absolutely sure about all statements made in your reports. Include any necessary verification with detailed analysis or other sources, preferably in the back of the report. Always anticipate questions the reader will ask and include the answers in the report.

   Even when a report is prepared by a subordinate, you will be judged by the accuracy of its content. So you must be able to ensure, directly or through experience and trust, that you can stand behind everything stated in the report.

2. *Double check math.* Make sure that all employees appreciate the importance of accuracy in math. Most business reports contain some level of numerical information. As a manager, you might find that you have a constant battle to get employees to appreciate the absolute need for 100 percent math accuracy.

   Problems might occur at the time a first draft is put together, or they can come up as a typing error. In either event, you must let employees know that any report containing even a single error is unacceptable.

3. *Check spelling.* Narrative sections of a report must also be as accurate as possible. A large number of people in the work force, even those with higher educations, have a problem with spelling. As a manager, you must recognize and accept that as an unfortunate fact of life. The problem, though, is not that some people cannot spell. It's in the lack of concern for accuracy.

   Set the standard for your department that all work is to be checked for spelling. Do not let anything leave your department without being subjected to editing. If necessary, assign one person who is a good speller to read over the reports prepared by others, looking for spelling errors and poor grammar. Make it your goal to produce reports that do not contain any errors at all. You will not achieve 100 percent accuracy in every case, but reducing errors to below the average will make your reports exceptional.

Your goal should not be to improve the spelling abilities of employees in your department, but to teach them that anything going out of the department represents them, and that they should care about the impression they create.

4. *Be aware of appearance.* The overall appearance of a report should be professional. It should have neatly spaced narrative sections, clear typing, and adequate margins. No one wants to read a report that consists of an endless narrative going from one edge of the paper to the other. The text should be broken up with indented or outlined sections, in-text graphics, and sub-heads.

These basic details collectively add to—or detract from—the perception of quality and professionalism of your department. You cannot assume that employees will even be aware that they make an impression with every document they send out. But you care about management's attitude toward your competence and ability. Remember that their attitudes are shaped by not only the content, but the appearance of your reports. A careless error or a poorly phrased sentence can make a big difference in how you are judged.

Lead by example. Draw up a sample report and distribute it to your employees. Be as clear as possible about your reporting standards, and point out on the sample what you expect them to do. If you expect employees to apply your standards, prepare your own reports meticulously and check your spelling, grammar, and math. Influence your employees and even other managers by setting examples for thorough research, thoughtful recommendations and conclusions, and intelligently written discussions.

You should have the reputation as a manager who insists on checking and checking again, who takes great care and pride in every document that comes from your department.

TRAINING SUBORDINATES

Delegating responsibility for a report to someone in your department is rarely an easy task. You cannot assume that an employee will automatically take the same care that you would. You will probably have to patiently remind subordinates of the need for fact verification and careful checking of reports and other forms of communication. You must demonstrate that you will consistently enforce those requirements. You must also monitor delegated work so that you can catch problems before the report is given to someone outside of the department.

In a busy department, you cannot spend all of your time doing reports, so you must be able to delegate effectively. But be sure you do not completely give up your supervisory responsibilities. Check the work that others have completed, and make sure your standards are being followed. If necessary, set the rule that nothing can leave the department without first being double-checked and approved. Hopefully, this will be only a temporary measure that you will be able to moderate later.

In respect to establishing standards for quality, both delegation and training are continuous functions, and you can't do them just once and then forget about them. Setting standards is only the beginning. You must then be able to enforce them, and you will need to remind employees of their own responsibilities.

You will discover that many employees will respond in the best possible way, by adopting your standards and performing brilliantly. Those are the employees with a successful future. But others will be unable to understand why quality is such an obsession for you. From their point of view, your insistence only makes their lives more difficult and they will never understand the value of creating the best possible impression.

Most alarming is that some employees are unaware that they have a problem. These employees probably don't even care about accuracy or appearance, not to mention the content of a report. They only want to get through a job as quickly and as easily as possible. You will find that the time required to supervise such employees is not worth the effort. There must be at least an attempt to improve and that requires acknowledgement of a problem.

These attitudes are not limited to entry-level employees. You will see people who feel this way at all levels of the organization. Rather than trying to change that attitude, you must learn to work around it and, ultimately, to rise above it. If you concentrate on your own standards for reporting and can lead the majority of your department in that direction, then you are surely on the way to a successful career.

MAKING YOUR PRESENTATION

Once you are able to produce accurate, concise reports that make a pleasing impression, you are ready to confront the dreaded presentation. You might be able to write many reports and send them through the company mail, but eventually you will be called into a meeting and asked to give an oral presentation as well.

If you have delegated the report to a subordinate and it contains misinterpreted information, errors, and other problems, your presentation will be a difficult one. You won't be able to answer questions and will make the worst possible impression. But if you prepare well, your presentation will be impressive, you will be able to answer every question with complete confidence, and you will gain the reputation as a dependable, professional, and knowledgeable employee.

Advance preparation and a complete knowledge of your material is essential to a successful presentation. If you experience stage fright, the best way to combat it is by being as prepared as possible in advance. In the next few sections are some tips for your preparation.

Outline Your Talk

Prepare an outline of the major points you plan to cover and write them on index cards. Then follow the outline, referring attendees to corresponding sections of the report.

Use Visual Aids

If your report includes charts and graphs, have them converted to transparencies (if your company can provide overhead projection) or use large copies. Use your visual aids as you make your presentation. If you have an especially severe case of stage fright, these graphics will help draw attention away from you during your speech.

Stay on the Most Important Topic

Don't expect to present your entire report. A verbal presentation should emphasize the most important points only. Follow the same sequence you use in the report—start with a summary, the conclusions, and your recommendations. Don't go into the details backing up these topics. If anyone has a question, you will be able to answer it in most cases by referring them to the relevant section of the report and then briefly explaining what's there.

Be Prepared for Questions

The listeners will probably have questions beyond those you anticipate. They might even interrupt your presentation to ask them. Don't let this throw you off. Give the answer and then proceed back to your outline. If you don't know the answer, don't try to bluff your way through it. You cannot be expected to know everything, especially if the question is not directly related to the report. Answer by saying, "I don't know, but I'll find out this afternoon and get right back to you."

Example: One manager uses these points to get through an especially difficult presentation. His company has been taken over by a large corporation, and the new management expects each manager to explain his or her department's function. There is considerable pressure, because everyone knows the new owners plan to cut some departments and to change the type of work some others do. Making a presentation under those conditions is not easy.

The manager writes a report and outlines his oral presentation keeping in mind the points listed above. He assumes that the most important question on the minds of the audience is, "Why should we leave your department intact?" So he designs his report to explain exactly what the department does, and how those activities are profitable to the company. His objective is to show that the savings resulting from his department's work justifies leaving it intact and perhaps even increasing the scope of its duties.

Some departments are consolidated or eliminated as a result of the review. But the manager who prepared so well is not only kept on the payroll; he also is given greater responsibilities and the total staff in his department is increased.

An oral presentation is a sales function. You must convince the listeners that your arguments are valid and that you understand the topic. To achieve this, you must be an expert on the subject you are discussing. Every report serves this function. You must sell your points to succeed and have your recommendations accepted. When you are faced with the prospect of having your department eliminated altogether, there is a lot of pressure to sell from desperation rather than knowledge. Resist that temptation in every report you prepare, whether oral or written, and you will achieve your objective most of the time.

REPORTS AND YOUR CAREER

Accept the idea that you are an expert about everything that goes on in your department. You would not be asked to prepare a report unless management already assumes this to be the case.

A mistake that some managers make is to assume that management always knows more than they do. When you are preparing information for someone else, do it with confidence in your own knowledge. No one can possibly know as much about your department as you do, so your report should contain an air of authority.

The greater your confidence, the better you will be perceived by management. That, together with your demonstrated ability to research a problem and present solutions, will make you a valuable manager.

Take a stand. Keeping quiet and going along with the way things are done when you have ideas for improvements is not the way to rise in your company. Promotions go to innovators and those who are willing to take calculated risks. While you should never go over your immediate supervisor's head or attempt to make policy on your own, you can and should have opinions and a voice. Management does not want a laundry list of problems. They want and need reports that tell them how to solve problems. Always address the concerns of management. Show them how to increase profits, cut costs and expenses, and reduce work loads.

Think of reports as your way of speaking up in the company, and be willing to accept risks that result in positive action. As long as your motives coincide with those of top management, the risks are not severe. Expressing ideas appropriately and well will bring you to the attention of your company's leadership. When promotions come up, they won't consider the cautious and conforming employee who is afraid to speak up, to take chances, or to question the traditional methods. They will want the individual who expresses ideas, presents solutions, and shows how suggestions can be put into action. The cautious employee might have a degree of job security. But if you are career-minded, you also know that you have to speak up to gain the recognition you deserve.

WORK PROJECT

1. You have delegated responsibility for a monthly report to an employee. The vice president sends one month's report back to you, with several spelling errors circled.

   a. What steps should you take to avoid this from recurring in the future?
   b. How can you improve your level of involvement and supervision without having to spend all of your time supervising the work of others?

2. Your department is responsible for a number of monthly reports. You notice that several have acceptable appearances, while others do not. How can you ensure that all reports will conform to the same standards?

3. At next week's executive board meeting, you are scheduled to give an oral presentation based on the proposal you submitted suggesting expansion of your department. What are three steps you can take to prepare?

Appendix A:
Work Project Answers

CHAPTER 1

1. Always prepare your report by identifying the likely questions the reader wants answered. In this case, the questions probably include:

a. Why are reports running late?
b. What can be done to correct the problem?
c. Is this problem likely to recur?
d. Are our original assumptions realistic?

2. When you generate a report on your own, you will not receive guidance from anyone else. You must add your own definition. The three important questions are:

a. Who is the reader? (Who will approve or reject your request?)
b. What is the reason? (*Why* should you be granted more floor space, and *how* will that improve efficiency or profits?)
c. What should the report contain? (You need to decide what facts, statistics, and other information are needed to prove your case and lead to approval.)

3. This request is a good example of an opportunity to make a specific recommendation. The summary section should state specifically what increases in expense and downtime have happened in recent months and what that trend shows. Your recommendations should state precisely which office machines should be replaced. And details should show the

trend of maintenance costs in terms of hours and dollars. These facts should support the conclusion you draw and the recommendations you make.

CHAPTER 2

1. The difficulty with the present format is that you cannot quickly find the answers you need. Suggest putting the summary on the first page of the report and following this with a listing of all recommendations. All supporting information should follow. Explain to the employee that while the details are important, your interest is in quickly getting to the answer of the question the report is addressing. Second, you need to see what recommendations are offered. And if you need to understand why and how those conclusions were drawn, you can then refer to the details.

2. This report does not ask for any interpretations or recommendations. It is a request to simply list information. Thus, the best format will consist of nothing more than account names or codes and the amounts. Another point: The accounting manager needs the report quickly to meet an early deadline. So this information should be prepared on a single page without any descriptions beyond the department name and the date.

3. Prepare the report in the improved format you want to propose, and submit it. Attach a memo explaining the changes and pointing out the advantages. Request approval of the change. If the idea is turned down, be prepared to prepare the report again, using the old format. If there is no response, assume your change is acceptable until told otherwise.

CHAPTER 3

1. A definition phase is usually first. In this case, you must determine whether the newsletter is to be typed or typeset, what method of printing will be used, how many copies will be run each month, how many pages each edition will contain, whether it will be one-color or multiple-color ink, and other specifics that will affect cost. Following

this, you will need to contact printers and typesetters in the area to get rough quotes on the cost of production. Finally, the report will summarize your findings. You may discover in some types of reports that the answers to your questions are not conclusive. In that case, prepare a report that gives comparative prices, and make a recommendation.

2. Being ahead of schedule gives you an advantage in the event a later phase is delayed. Don't promise to deliver a report early, however. Once you make that promise, you lose reputation if you can't come through. It's better to deliver it early without having made the promise, or to use the time to do more research than you thought you'd have time for.

3. You should always be concerned if a lengthy report is underway. Keep the lines of communication open by requesting status review meetings. This avoids the all-too-common problem of ending up with a report different from what was asked for originally.

CHAPTER 4

1. Keeping in mind that the reader is interested in discovering the most important information, first summarize the numbers, ·then include needed details:

Total expenses for the month were $6,319, or 10% over budget. The most significant unfavorable variance occurred in the travel and entertainment account. A summary of variances:

Account	Expense	Variance
Travel, Ent.	$ 4,587	− 14.7%
Office	682	− 7.9
Postage	218	+27.3
Printing	832	− 4.0

2. Be especially aware of rambling sentences that contain too many large words. Strive for the simple and direct approach. For example, this could be rewritten as:

A 32% increase in transactions over the last six months points out the need for upgrades to our system. We recommend the purchase or lease of three more terminals in the department.

3. Reducing a paragraph that lists steps to outline form clarifies what you're trying to say. This paragraph could be rewritten as:

> Input is done directly from invoices. The following procedure is in effect:
>
> 1. The supervisor approves each invoice for payment.
> 2. Cross-footing is checked.
> 3. Invoices are matched to the requisition.
> 4. A code is assigned for the expense or, when needed, a series of codes.
> 5. A batch total is added for verification following input.

CHAPTER 5

1. The significance of the information is not reflected by the report. Month-to-month comparisons might be of value to the reader, but you should expand the report's format to include a comparison to the previous year as well. Also comment on seasonal variations in the level of sales, so that the reader has a greater appreciation of month-to-month changes.

2. The arrangement of information is the reverse of what the reader needs. Put the conclusion and recommendation up front, including the financial results of studies and estimates you have completed. Then support that information with details in the body of the report.

3. A long-standing format is one the reader is accustomed to seeing. If you change that format without approval, expect resistance. The best solution is to prepare the report in the new format. Also write out the advantages of the changes you're proposing and the disadvantages with the old format. Submit these to your supervisor for approval, and recommend submitting the new and improved version if the report goes elsewhere.

CHAPTER 6

1. The danger in trying to put too much information on one graph is that it will confuse rather than enlighten the reader. Consider prepar-

ing a vertical bar graph for each division, being sure to use the same scale for each. Then, for the current period only, show all divisions on a single bar graph.

2. The graph actually shows a percentage increase, but the title might mislead someone to think it is a summary of actual net profits. The title should read, "Percentage Change in Office Supply Expenses, One Year." Your caption should further clarify exactly what the graph shows. For example: "This is a summary of percentage increases from one month to the next, for the past full year."

3. To prepare a circle graph, you must convert percentages to degrees. A full circle contains 360 degrees. Multiply each percentage by 360, and round to the closest full degree:

$$
\begin{array}{rcrcr}
38\% & \times & 360 & = & 137 \\
24 & \times & 360 & = & 86 \\
16 & \times & 360 & = & 58 \\
17 & \times & 360 & = & 61 \\
5 & \times & 360 & = & 18 \\
\end{array}
$$

Total degrees   360

CHAPTER 7

1. With six months of financial information to report, a strictly narrative explanation will not clarify what's happening in this account. And putting the facts in chart form forces you to discuss the trend in a separate narrative section. The unfavorable variance is fairly consistent each month, indicating that the original budget was not accurate enough for the level of activity. To show this consistent trend, consider a line graph that shows the level of the budget and actual. This graph can be incorporated into text. Discuss the consistency of the trend and investigate the original budget to determine the cause of the problem. Then recommend actions that should be taken (such as revising the current budget or, if appropriate, initiating expense controls).

2. Ratios are generally short numerical statements. They are perfectly suited for inclusion in text, and can be highlighted in the middle of a paragraph in the manner shown in the "Making Reports Readable" section. Even a large number of ratios can be handled in this way.

Narratives should be devoted to explanations of the trend each ratio represents.

3. Show the progress of all jobs in one place. Consider starting the report with an overview, including graphic summaries and brief explanations. Then the rest of the report can be devoted to examining the causes of those projects that are behind schedule. For this type of report, an annotated or footnoted graph will be most appropriate, since the schedule can be best shown in a left-to-right format. Major causes of delays can be effectively highlighted on the graph itself, with more detailed narratives included before or after.

CHAPTER 8

1. The outline form should clearly identify responsibility and the order of steps. For example:

> Part-time employees complete time reports and submit them to the department manager no later than 10 a.m. each Friday. The manager follows these steps:

1. Check time reports to make sure they are completely filled out (see attached sample).
2. If time reports are not complete, return them to the employee.
3. Review time reported with the weekly schedule, verifying accuracy.
4. If time is questioned, review with the employee.
5. Make changes as needed.
6. Check math on corrected time report.
7. Make changes as needed.
8. Sign the report, approving payment.
9. Forward approved time reports to the payroll department for payment.

2. A vertical flowchart should identify each of the steps and decision points. For example:

Steps	*Decision Points*
1. Time reports submitted.	Complete?
2. If incomplete, return to employee.	
3. Compare for accuracy.	Accurate?
4. Discuss with employee.	
5. Make changes.	
6. Check math.	Math correct?
7. Make changes.	
8. Sign reports.	
9. Forward for payment.	

3. A horizontal flowchart of the same procedure will expand the report. Areas of responsibility are the employee, the manager, and the payroll department. The employee is involved only at the beginning (when reports are submitted) and if and when questions arise or errors are found—the decision points. The time line should indicate the 10 A.M. Friday deadline and the final time deadline for sending approved time cards to the payroll department (the last step). And the time report itself is the only form included in the procedure.

CHAPTER 9

1. Both reports deal with the same information, but present it in different formats. This is a common problem, but the solution is a simple one.

a. The reports can be improved by combining them into one single report. The information should be shown in both formats. This will take nothing away from either of the previous reports and could even be of greater value to both departments needing the information.

b. Providing more information for less work will not require permission in most cases. You should be able to institute the change on your own. Assume you have the authority to improve on the format of reports you prepare in your department.

2. The size of this report can be reduced by concentrating on areas needing management's attention—those projects falling behind schedule. The ones on schedule can be explained in one sentence: "All other projects are on schedule, and no problems are anticipated in the future."

3. The danger is that, in eliminating names from your distribution list, someone will feel threatened by the exclusion. Someone might need to use the report. You cannot simply assume that someone does not need it, without first inquiring. The best way to remove names from the list is to offer them the choice. Rather than suggesting that they should no longer get the report, ask whether they *want* to continue receiving it.

CHAPTER 10

1. Delegation must be balanced with a degree of supervision so that reports don't go out with obvious errors. The solution:

a. Make sure that no reports are sent out from your department until all math, spelling, and other points are checked.
b. Delegate the responsibility of checking reports to employees in the department, especially those who are exceptionally dependable and thorough.

2. Draft a sample report in the standard format. Instruct employees to follow that format in every case. Avoid inconsistency of style and quality in reports so that those who receive and read them know what to expect from you.

3. Oral presentations of a report can be especially intimidating. Prepare in advance by outlining what you plan to say. Use visual aids to emphasize the major issues, and anticipate questions listeners are likely to ask.

Appendix B:

Sample Report—The Narrative Form

Hanson Research Corporation
Proposal: Upgrade of Internal Systems

[This fictitious company provides its customers with research services. For example, one major client requests demographic studies and product test marketing.]

[Cover Memo]

This is a proposal for an upgrade of internal systems involving the automation of our customer data base. The proposal concerns two primary areas: word processing and customer service. A complete conversion can be achieved within six months from approval date.

We contend that the cost of automating in these two areas will be justified by the improvement in efficiency and response, both to customers and in the development of printed material. While our study did not include other areas, we are certain that the availability of automation will prove advantageous to several other departments.

To develop our conclusions, we analyzed the current methods of work completion and trends in the volume of work. The volume of gross income over the last three years has increased by 325%. Yet, we continue to type reports manually. Given the nature of the work (the need for several revisions to a report, for example), our product is perfectly suited to word processing.

This report was undertaken jointly by three people: the managers of accounting (primary responsibility), customer service, and the typing pool.

RECOMMENDATIONS

A: Major Conclusions

The analysis of our current system, coupled with an investigation of available systems, leads us to the following conclusions:

1. The service we provide to customers is ideally suited to automation. With current manual processing methods, the level of work load increases in proportion to the volume of gross income. That condition will be modified through automation.
2. Continuing to develop reports on typewriters is no longer the most efficient alternative.
3. Volume has increased 325% in three years. This has created a significantly higher work load for the typing pool and for the customer service department. Yet, staffing in these areas has grown by only 42% during the three-year period.
4. Continuing to use existing systems will require additional staffing over the next three years to an extent that exceeds the cost of automation.
5. Automated systems will not completely eliminate the need for additional employees. However, it will (a) improve efficiency and turnaround time, and (b) slow down the budgeted rate of growth in staff.
6. The full cost of automating the two areas studied will be $79,300, based on average costs on the market today.

Software (shelf product)	$ 2,300
Software (custom)	25,000
Hardware	42,000
Training	10,000
Total	$79,300

7. The company will recover this investment within two years from full conversion (or 2.5 years from approval date), just in terms of staffing. This does not include the intangible benefits of improved efficiency and response time.
8. Additional benefits of automation will be discovered as other departments begin to place their systems on computer.

B: Action Plan

Based on the conclusions of our research, we offer the following recommended course of action:

Recommendation	*Proposed Deadline*
1. Compare costs of available word processing software systems.	2 weeks
2. Compare costs of available word processing and computer hardware. (We recommend purchase of computers rather than dedicated word processors so that use will not be limited to one function.)	4 weeks
3. Compare the availability of training with purchase of systems.	4 weeks
4. Purchase hardware and software and commence internal training.	8 weeks
5. Convert from manual to automated processing of reports.	12 weeks
6. Define criteria for customer service data base	15 weeks
7. Enter an agreement for the development of custom software for customer service.	18 weeks
8. Install complete system.	26 weeks

SUPPORT

A: Current Work Methods

Typing Pool

The 11 employees in this department currently process reports on electric typewriters. Account executives or employees in the research departments forward various segments of reports to the typing pool with indicated deadlines.

Upon completion of initial drafts, photocopies of reports are forwarded to account executives for review. Changes are made to the drafts and returned to the typing pool for correction.

This review process may involve three or more revisions to copy. Depending upon the scope of changes, large sections of each report are invariably retyped at least twice.

Customer Service

Customers call the department with questions, most of which have to do with the current status of projects. Under the present system, representatives must check with account executives and return phone calls to the customer.

There is no centralized customer data base and no internal provision for reporting progress on jobs underway. The department has files for each customer and for each job; however, the files are only as current as the latest contact with account executives, many of whom are located in other offices.

B: Gross Income Analysis

The company has experienced the following levels of gross income over the last three years:

Year	Income
1986	$1,450,000
1987	3,835,000
1988	6,162,000

Based on the current year's forecast and discussions with the vice president of marketing, we estimate the next three years' gross income as:

Year	Income
1989	$8,300,000
1990	9,000,000
1991	9,800,000

Even a conservative increase in the current level of volume will have a direct impact on both the typing pool and the customer service department. There must be a proportionate increase in staffing in both of these areas, since we provide a personalized service.

C: Staffing Analysis

Both departments studied for this report have had increases in staff over the last three years. However, the combined increase has been only 42%, compared with a 325% increase in volume for the same period:

	Staffing		
	1986	1987	1988
Typing pool	7	8	11
Customer service	5	5	6

On the basis of the current budget and estimates for the coming three years, we estimate staffing growth as follows (based on the assumption that the current system is left intact):

	Staffing		
	1989	1990	1991
Typing pool	13	15	18
Customer service	8	10	11

The anticipated need for staff increases must be reviewed with floor-space restrictions in mind. Our headquarters' office is currently near full capacity. The area occupied by the typing pool could handle an additional three employees and work stations (we conservatively estimate a need for seven more in the next three years). And the customer service area is already crowded. We expect the need for an additional five employees over the next three years.

D: Cost Analysis

We researched the cost of software, hardware, and training with several sources on the market. A contributor to this effort was one of our company's account executives who has performed similar research jobs for customers. On the basis of that research (detailed analysis and vendor sales literature is available upon request), we have estimated total costs:

1. Software (Existing)

Existing word processing software is recommended. Several versatile and affordable systems are on the market, and there should be no need to duplicate these with custom software. The requirements of the typing pool are for the management of files and not for any specific functions unique to our organization.

Based on a survey of 18 manufacturers, we estimate the cost of word processing software at $2,300.

2. Software (Custom)

Our customer service department's needs are more specialized than those of the typing pool's. We recommend creation of a customer data base that will include name, address, phone, contact names, a description section, historical job records, and up to five schedules (for current projects). A separate preliminary analysis was performed to identify the required data capacity of a system, based on estimates of volume over the next three years. This study has dictated the requirements of software and hardware.

Based on interviews with custom software sources, we estimate the cost of development at $25,000.

3. Hardware

We estimate the need for one high-speed letter-quality printer and 20 terminal work stations (15 in the typing pool and 5 in the customer service department), in addition to other hardware components.

Proposals submitted by 9 manufacturers indicate the cost will be approximately $42,000. (All proposals and other materials submitted by hardware manufacturers are available upon request.)

4. Training

We specified that both software and hardware suppliers must include initial training. All proposals included in our study include externally provided training as part of the cost. However, we believe that internal conversion from manual to automated processing will require additional expense.

Based on discussions with managers in each department, and with the consulting account executive, we have added $10,000 to our estimated total cost.

Summary

Software (shelf product)	$ 2,300
Software (customized)	25,000
Hardware	42,000
Training	10,000
Total	$79,300

E: Cost Recovery Analysis

We estimate that it will require two years from full conversion for the company to recover its initial costs. This estimate is based solely on salaries and wages and does not include an allowance for secondary benefits.

Employees in the typing pool are currently paid an average of $11.50 per hour. Due to increased work load and the methods currently in use, we have experienced substantial overtime, particularly during the past year. Total salaries and wages for the next three years (assuming an average number of salary increases and that no changes are made in the current system) are estimated as:

1989	1990	1991
$313,500	$360,000	$450,000

With automation of the typing pool, we estimate comparative costs on the following assumptions:

- With conversion time, no change is made for the first year.
- It will be possible to modify estimated staff levels to:

1989	1990	1991
13	13	14

- Greater skill levels will result in an accelerated average hourly rate (this estimate is based on the market rate for word processing professionals) to $13.50 per hour (in two years) and $15 per hour (in three years).
- We estimate that overtime will be eliminated because of improvements in systems.

With these assumptions in effect, our estimated salaries in the typing pool are:

1989	1990	1991
$313,500	$342,200	$409,500

Employees in the customer service department are currently paid average salaries of $19,500 per year. The total of salaries in this department for the next three years (assuming that the current system is left unchanged and an average number of salary increases are granted) will be:

1989	1990	1991
$156,000	$200,000	$229,000

We estimate that with an improved system it will be possible to reduce anticipated staff levels to:

1989	1990	1991
8	9	9

Our estimate of salaries over the coming three years assumes no change during the first year (due to the time required for conversion):

1989	1990	1991
$156,000	$185,000	$195,000

Summary

Estimate of future salaries, assuming that change is made to the current system:

	1989	1990	1991
Typing pool	$313,500	$360,000	$450,000
Customer service	156,000	200,000	229,000
Total	$469,500	$560,000	$679,000

Estimate of future salaries, if conversion is made to automated processing:

	1989	1990	1991
Typing pool	$313,500	$342,200	$409,500
Customer service	156,000	185,000	195,000
Total	$469,500	$527,200	$604,500
Total savings	$ 0	$ 32,800	$ 74,500

Recovery of the company's investment in an automated system will occur in approximately two years from the date the new system becomes operational (2.5 years from approval date). We believe that the ongoing cost of computer supplies and maintenance will be greater than the current cost for supplies and maintenance of electric typewriters. However, this factor is offset by other benefits of changing systems.

F: Intangible Benefits

Our analysis extends only for the next three years. By automating now, we will create a system that will hold down future salary costs and, at the same time, increase our capacity for fast turnaround and response to customers. While the fixed cost of maintaining an automated system will level out, the benefits will accrue for many years to come.

Risk to the organization is limited. All managers interviewed for this proposal agree that efficiency will improve and salary expenses will be reduced over the next three years. Costs of the new system will be recovered tangibly within a short period of time.

Under current procedures, a moderate level of change to a report (for errors, new sections, or reorganization of material) consumes an average of 13 hours in the typing pool. Most of this time is spent retyping. Use of a word processing system is estimated to reduce this time to less than four hours per redraft. In addition, changes can be made to existing files. Presently, a single change on a page often requires a redraft of the entire page.

Improved turnaround will have a secondary benefit of enabling account executives to personally respond to customers, to stay within schedule, and to be more productive.

Customer service responses will be more efficient, assuming that current schedules will be updated on a recurring basis once automation is in place. Even remotely located executives will have the ability to access data files by telephone under the proposal analysis prepared for this report. The cost estimates include this capability. Thus, service representatives will be able to more knowledgeably respond to customer inquiries.

G: Advantages to Other Departments

In addition to the typing pool and customer service, other departments will benefit from the availability of automation. The data base requirements of the customer service department will also facilitate a variety of applications in other departments. For example:

Accounting
- Accounts receivable and billings
- Check issue
- General ledger
- Expense budgets

Marketing
- Tracking of volume
- Market planning
- Market plan and forecasting

These systems would require additional investment in software and the purchase of more terminals. However, the investment in hardware will have been made as part of this initial cost analysis and recommendation. So the actual cost to acquire automated system improvements will be minimal for other departments.

Appendix C:

Sample Report—The Financial Form

Adams Equity Group, Inc.
Analysis of Production

[*This fictitious company sells investments, insurance, and advisory services to individuals and corporate clients. Branch offices are independent affiliates.*]

[*Cover Memo*]

This report summarizes annual production among branch offices for the year just ended. Its purpose is to demonstrate regions of substantial production and also to indicate areas below minimum volume standards.

The analysis was divided between branch offices that have (a) been affiliated with the company for more than one year and (b) been affiliated for less than one year. We have observed significant differences in average volume levels between these two groups.

During the year, 46% of our branch offices (including only those offices affiliated with the company for one year or more) were responsible for 91 percent of total production. Of a total of 186 branches, 77, or 41 percent of our offices, are located in three of the 38 states in which the company operates; they were responsible for 54 percent of total production.

We found that, of 44 new branch offices joining the firm during the year, 11 accounted for 73 percent of new branch office production.

RECOMMENDATIONS

On the basis of results for the year and their significance in terms of home office support costs, we make the following recommendations:

1. This report should be prepared on a quarterly basis from this point forward. Trends in branch offices should be monitored throughout the year, and negative trends dealt with immediately.
2. A market tracking system should be developed and followed to encourage higher levels of production in those branches falling below average. A proposed system has been developed in preliminary form and is enclosed in a separate report.
3. We recommend a sliding scale of commissions based on attainment of acceptable levels of production. A preliminary policy change is included in the separate market tracking proposal.
4. The company should establish and enforce minimum production standards for branch offices joining the firm. The large number of offices currently affiliated that do not generate acceptable levels of volume are creating losses for the company. For example, gross volume for the year was 14 percent above the previous year; net profits were 32 percent lower.
5. The company should consider reducing or eliminating its presence in states other than California, Oregon, and Washington. For the last three years, branch offices in the home state and the two other Pacific states have accounted for the majority of gross volume. In support of this idea, we point out that:
    a. Home office support of remote offices is more expensive than it is for those closer to our own location.
    b. Production levels are consistently lower in remote branch offices than in offices closer to the home office.
    c. The production trend being reported has been consistent for the last three years.

SUPPORT

A: Production Levels

Affiliated one year or more: (1)	Branch Offices		Production	
	Number	%	($000)	%
Volume over $500,000	14	10%	$ 9,512	31%
Volume $250–$500,000	51	36	18,430	60
Subtotal (2)	65	46%	$27,942	91%
Volume under $250,000	77	54	2,884	9
Total	142	100%	$30,826	100%

Affiliated less than one year: (1)	Branch Offices		Production	
	Number	%	($000)	%
Volume over $500,000	2	5%	$1,492	22%
Volume $250–$500,000	9	20	3,411	51
Subtotal (3)	11	25%	$4,903	73%
Volume under $250,000	33	75	1,840	27
Total (4)	44	100%	$6,743	100%

Total production (1)	Branch Offices		Production	
	Number	%	($000)	%
Volume over $500,000	16	9%	$11,004	29%
Volume $250–$500,000	60	32	21,841	58
Subtotal (5)	76	41%	$32,845	87%
Volume under $250,000	110	59	4,724	13
Total (6)	186	100%	$37,569	100%

Notes:

(1) All production is reported on a cash basis, with income booked as received.
(2) Of branch offices affiliated with the company for one year or more, 46% of branches generated 91% of production.

(3) Of branch offices affiliated with the company for less than one year, 25% of branches generated 73% of production.

(4) These branch offices joined the company during the year. Reported production is not for a full 12-month period.

(5) Overall, 41% of branch offices reported 87% of the year's production.

(6) A total of 186 branch offices produced $37.569 million for the year, for an average per branch office of $201,984.

B: Regional Analysis

Region	Branch Offices	Production ($000)	Average ($000)
California (1)			
Los Angeles	19	$ 5,215	$274
San Diego	11	2,558	233
San Francisco	9	2,542	282
Washington (1)			
Seattle	14	3,452	247
Spokane	10	2,563	256
Oregon (1)			
Portland	8	2,168	271
Salem	6	1,713	286
Rocky Mountains	5	1,018	204
Arizona	7	1,344	192
Texas	11	2,046	186
Midwest	22	3,626	165
Pennsylvania	10	1,820	182
New England	16	2,448	153
Virginia	4	648	162
Florida	16	2,198	137
South	18	2,210	123
Total	186	$37,569	$202

Note:

(1) Summary of volume for the three Pacific states:

Region	Offices	%	Production	%
California	39	21%	$10,315	28%
Washington	24	13	6,015	16
Oregon	14	7	3,881	10
Subtotal	77	41	$20,211	54
All other	109	59	17,358	46
Total	186	100%	$37,569	100%

Appendix D:

Sample Report—The Combined Form

Todd Design Associates
Printing Expense Control Proposal

[*This fictitious company is staffed with designers and architects, and offers space planning and office design services to corporate customers.*]

[*Cover Memo*]

The purpose of this report is to analyze the causes of continued unfavorable variances in printing expenses. Over the last 24 months, although the organization has experienced significant growth in volume and customer base, outside printing has consistently exceeded the budget.

A review of the budget itself reveals no obvious flaws. That budget has been increased each year in anticipation of higher costs for printing. Yet, the actual expenses continue to exceed the budget.

Our analysis demonstrates the need for direct and centralized control and preapproval over printing jobs requested by various departments.

This report was prepared by the manager of the marketing department, upon request by the president.

RECOMMENDATIONS

1. Centralize responsibility for ordering outside printing. Modify current procedures for requisitioning so that one individual can combine jobs, compare prices, and determine appropriate run levels.
2. Establish a revised budget level for printing.
3. Track the success of the new procedure.

SUPPORT

A: The Current Procedure

Each department orders its own printing from a number of local shops. With many people involved, there is no consistent practice of comparison pricing, and we give up the leverage of requesting a consolidated printing job from one shop.

For example, during the month of July, five individuals ordered printing jobs from the outside. The marketing and accounting departments had forms and letterhead printed. And managers of three projects also requested reproduction of specifications and plans. The total cost for the month was $1,930, compared with a budget of $1,200.

The similarity of printing jobs for the three projects during the month points out a missed opportunity. By combining these requests and comparing prices, we would have been

Marketing	$ 619
Accounting	407
Job 615	285
Job 680	370
Job 722	249
July total	$ 1,930

able to save part of this cost. For example, we asked for bids from four printers for the three jobs, if they had been submitted at the same time. Total cost of doing the jobs separately was $904 (above). Printers give substantial discounts for submission of work

Bid 1	$750
Bid 2	718
Bid 3	685
Bid 4	715
Median	$717
Savings	$187

at the same time. In this instance, we would have saved about $187 by combining the three jobs into one printing request. An additional reason for the lower overall cost relates to selection of the best printer for a particular job. Two of the three jobs run during the month were given to print shops specializing in high-quality jobs. We would be likely to use them for letterhead, marketing brochures, and multi-color printing. However, we required only one-sided, one-color reproduction services in these cases, and these shops did not give the best price.

The individual project managers are not to blame for this situation. They know they can depend on timely delivery and quality work from a printer they have used in the past. In the absence of a centralized procedure for ordering printing, department and project managers have no choice but to contract for their work individually. Their job should not be to expertly compare prices, because time constraints make such considerations a luxury. Rather, this should be the job of one individual who understands the availability and quality of services and who can combine work to obtain the best possible price.

It may not be practical to combine work in all cases. For example, two project managers might need work on dissimilar deadlines. In that case, combining the jobs would require delaying one. That is not proposed. We suggest that whenever possible we should reduce the cost of printing through coordinated responsibility and control.

B: Suggested Change in Procedure

The solution to this problem will involve centralizing responsibility for obtaining printing. This will produce several advantages:

- Knowledge of different rates
- Reduced rates for combined jobs
- Singular responsibility for volume of orders

We suggest that the marketing department be given responsibility for ordering printing jobs from the outside. The order form currently in use can serve as a requisition without any need for changes.

The marketing department is a logical choice for this responsibility. This department orders more printing than any other department and, as part of its duties, has developed a broader knowledge of printing policies and prices than other departments.

Steps in the suggested procedure include:

1. Individual department and project managers complete the requisition form and submit it to the marketing department.

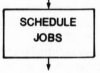

2. The marketing department schedules print jobs on the basis of deadlines and the nature of the jobs.

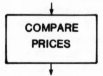

3. Price comparisons will be made on the basis of the number of similar jobs to be printed at the same time.

4. Materials will be delivered to printers by the marketing department.

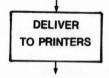

5. All completed jobs will be returned directly to the marketing department.

6. Marketing will examine work to ensure the quality of the job. When necessary, work will be returned to the printer for re-runs.

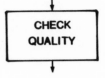

7. Acceptable work will be delivered to the individual department manager. The marketing department is responsible for meeting agreed-upon deadlines.

8. The marketing department will keep accurate records of departmental or project job costs, and will summarize coding for the accounting department each month.

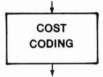

9. The marketing department will track costs and compare them to budget. A monthly summary report will be prepared and submitted to management in time for the budget review meeting.

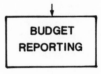

Appendix E:

Punctuation and Usage Quick-Check

INTRODUCTION

The following section presents recommendations and guidelines for many of the common problems you will encounter in punctuation and usage. If you supervise a diverse staff of employees, one of the problems you face is establishing a logical and consistent set of rules. This is because:

1. English is less than precise.
2. Employees have different cultural and educational backgrounds.
3. Companies' rules and practices vary.
4. Employees are inconsistent in following rules of usage.
5. Standards for business letters continually change.

Some organizations develop their own style and usage guidelines, although in many cases the question of consistency is not addressed formally. Rules are devised in departments without uniform guidelines or written policies. If your company doesn't have written standards, it is up to you to develop guidelines on your own. The following recommendations will help you in training your staff, establishing standards, and enforcing them.

The appendix includes these sections:

Punctuation hints: the forms of punctuation and their proper usage.
Good usage guidelines: recommendations for setting standards for
   abbreviations, capitalization, numbers, percents, and underlining.
Commonly misused words: words that are frequently misused and
   their proper definitions.
Commonly misspelled words: words that have spelling variations or
   are frequently misspelled.
Useful references: books that offer you additional help.

You will not be able to identify the "right" way to express a thought
in every case. Form and usage guidelines should be thought of as
recommendations only, to be used to set standards for consistency. If
your organization does not publish its own guidelines, recommend that
a written policy be established to handle questions of style and usage.

PUNCTUATION HINTS

apostrophe   Use in contracted words *(don't, doesn't)* and in possessives
(John's report, the company's standard, workers' rights).

asterisk   Used to footnote or annotate a reference that (1) does not fit
in the thought or (2) is a secondary idea.

> The loss for the year* also reduced the market's perception of
> future growth potential.
> *The loss was due to a one-time extraordinary adjustment.

bar   Also called the slant or slash, the bar is used in place of a
conjunction *(and, or)*.

> the April/May/June quarter

brackets   Indicates material added in a quotation that is not part of the
quote.

> He went along with [the proposal].

colon   Use with a short list, a salutation, or time of day.

> We use two versions: current and year-to-date.
>
> Dear Mr. Smith:
>
> 3:30 p.m.

comma   Offsets a second thought in a sentence, interrupts a primary thought, distinguishes two unrelated ideas in one sentence, separates a series of words or phrases, or divides adjectives. Also used within numbers, dates, city and state names, to precede a short quotation, and to add clarity between two unrelated numbers.

> The department, newly formed last year, reports to the vice president.
>
> The report, though, was not correct.
>
> He plans to attend the meeting, which promises to be a productive one.
>
> Offices are located in New York, San Francisco, Chicago, St. Louis, and Los Angeles.
>
> It was a clear, focused letter.
>
> We earned $18,456,000 last year.
>
> December 15, 1988
>
> Atlanta, Georgia
>
> He answered, "Yes, by Monday."
>
> During 1988, 14 employees were hired.

dash   Offsets a separate thought. (On a typewriter, use double hyphen.)

> Letters—other than those written in response to an extended list of questions—should be limited to one page.
>
> The manager—normally a capable employee—made significant errors in the report.

ellipsis   Used to indicate deletions in a quotation, a pause, or an incomplete thought. When the ellipsis occurs within the sentence, use three periods; at the end of the sentence, use four (one for the period and three for the ellipsis).

"They . . . met with the board."

The decision was delayed . . . and then delayed again.

If only we'd met beforehand. . . .

exclamation mark   Ends a sentence with emphasis. Usage in business letters should be rare.

They reversed their position again!

Now they say we never wrote to them!

hyphen   Used to connect related words:

year-to-date

go-between

ready-made

short- and long-term

parenthesis   Used as an alternative to commas or dashes to separate an unrelated thought within a sentence, to expand on a preceding statement, to refer to a source, for abbreviations after a full name or title, or to offset elements of an outline or a list.

The report (on production) was sent to every manager.

Mr. Adams (vice president of operations) was in attendance.

Production declined by 14% (figures supplied by the marketing department).

Internal Revenue Service (IRS)

(a) sick days

    (b) vacation
    (c) holidays

period   Marks the end of a sentence or abbreviation. Examples of use in abbreviations:

et cetera	etc.
Incorporated	Inc.
February	Feb.
Mister	Mr.
Monday	Mon.

question mark   Signifies the end of an interrogatory statement. As a general rule, don't use more than one, although occasional use for emphasis is acceptable:

    What does this mean??

quotation marks   Used for direct quotes or to indicate slang or jargon. For a quote within a quote, use single quotation marks.

    He said, "The check was mailed to you this morning."

    He insisted on "data integrity" in the report.

    He argued, "I heard them say 'Stop' so I waited."

semicolon   Used to distinguish multiple thoughts within one sentence.

    The report contained a summary; supplements from divisions four, seven, and nine; and recommendations.

GOOD USAGE GUIDELINES

abbreviations   Should be used in a complete sentence only when part of a name or title.

    [Correct]
    Mr. Smith is president of the company.

[Incorrect]

Mr. Smith is pres. of the co.

Follow shortened words with a period, but avoid periods within abbreviations. For example, "IRS" is preferred over "I.R.S."

capitalization   The first word of every sentence is to be capitalized (including a complete thought following a colon), as are all proper nouns and abbreviations of organizations.

This is the report we promised.

This belongs to the Boston branch office.

We sent the return to the IRS.

It was simple: He didn't complete the job.

Capitalization can also be used to emphasize a key word or phrase, although be careful of overuse.

numbers   Write out the number if under 10, abbreviate if 10 or more. When a single sentence contains mixed usage, express all in figures.

We have five months until the deadline.

Include all 12 months in the report.

Only 5 of the 12 months show a variance.

Regardless of the first rules, numbers appearing at the beginning of a sentence should *always* be spelled out:

Thirty-five employees have been hired.

Avoid mixing numerical systems.

[Wrong]

The IX Section reported 11 new jobs.

[Right]

Section Four reported 11 new jobs.

Do not use ordinal numbers ("1st," "2nd") in the text of a letter.

> *[Wrong]*
>
> We reported a 2nd quarter profit.
>
> *[Right]*
>
> We reported a second-quarter profit.

Ordinals are acceptable in street addresses and sometimes in tabular material.

percent   We recommend spelling out "percent" when used without a corresponding number; use the symbol when part of a number (14%).

underlining   Used to indicate emphasis as with italics, in reference sections of letters, or to highlight sections of an outline.

> We <u>must</u> meet the deadline.
>
> Subject: <u>Smith vs. Hanson Corp.</u>
>
> Section III: <u>Market Analysis</u>

COMMONLY MISUSED WORDS

accept   to receive
except   to exclude

advice   an opinion
advise   to offer an opinion or information

affect   to influence
effect   to create or cause; a result

allude   to imply or state indirectly
elude   to avoid or escape

allusion   a reference to another subject
illusion   a false belief or appearance

already   by now
all ready   everyone or everything is ready

altogether   completely
all together   everyone or everything

among   with three or more
between   with two

ascent   rise
assent   permission

beside   next to
besides   in addition to

biannual   twice a year
biennial   every two years

can   is able
may   has permission

complement   a piece that provides completion
compliment   praise

conscious   aware of
conscience   awareness of right and wrong

continual   in succession
continuous   without stop

council   a committee or group
counsel   to give suggestions or advice; an attorney

credible   likely or believable
creditable   admirable or deserving

definite   absolute
definitive   conclusive or exact

detract   to take away
distract   to harass or preoccupy

discreet   prudent
discrete   separate

each other   two
one another   more than two

eminent   noteworthy
imminent   impending

extant   intact, preserved
extent   degree

farther   reference to measurable distance
further   in addition to

forego   go before
forgo   go without

in   within
into   in reference to entering

incredible   not to be believed
incredulous   skeptical

ingenious   skilled, able
ingenuous   candid

interstate   between different states
intrastate   within one state

last   the final
latest   the most recent

later   after
latter   the second of two things

lay   to put down
lie   to recline

may be   a verb implying possibility
maybe   an adverb meaning perhaps

persecute   to chase or harass
prosecute   to bring legal action

practical   of use
practicable   possible

precede   to come before
proceed   to go forward

principal   of higher rank
principle   truth or idea

respectful   with respect
respective   in regard to

set   to place
sit   to assume a sitting position

stationary   unmoving
stationery   supplies for the office

COMMONLY MISSPELLED WORDS

English spelling, like punctuation and usage, is not subject to consistent or constant rules. Many words have spelling variations, and not every dictionary is in agreement on what is correct. The following list contains the recommended spelling for words that have variations and the correct spelling for words that are commonly misspelled.

absence	accessible	accommodate
achievement	acknowledgment	acquire
addenda	advantageous	adviser
advisory	affect	affidavit
aggrieved	all right	analogous
analysis	analyze	anomaly
apparent	argument	auxiliary
belief	believe	beneficial
benefited	bona fide	by-product
calendar	caliber	cancelled
cancellation	catalog	category
coming	commitment	comparative

concede
controversy
coordinate
correctable
crystallize
definitely
description
diagrammatic
discernible
effect
eminent
encyclopedia
exaggerate
existent
facetious
feasibility
forcibly
fulfill
glamorous
grievance
hierarchical
idiosyncrasy
indefatigable
inert
intellect
judgment
juvenile
knowledgeable
liaison
likable
maintenance
maneuver
measurable
misspell
necessitate
nonplussed
nucleus
obsolete

conscious
controversial
copyright
correlation
curriculums
definition
device
dilapidated
disk
eligible
employee
entrust
excellence
experience
farfetched
fictitious
foreword
gamut
glamour
harass
hierarchy
imminence
independent
inquiry
interest
judiciary
juxtapose
led
licensee
linear
manageable
marriage
medieval
naive
negligent
noticeable
obsession
occasion

consensus
cooperate
corollary
counselor
defense
describe
diagrammed
disastrous
echelon
embarrass
enclose
environment
excerpt
explanation
fascinate
focused
formulas
gauge
glossary
height
hodgepodge
impatient
indispensable
inspector
jeopardize
juncture
keypunch
leveling
licensor
losing
mandatory
marshaled
mileage
necessary
negligible
notwithstanding
obsolescence
occur

occurred	occurrence	occurring
offbeat	offhanded	oftentimes
opinion	opportunity	paid
paralyze	particular	penetrate
perceptible	performance	permanent
personal	personnel	persuasive
phraseology	possible	practical
practice	precede	predicate
predominant	preempt	preexisting
prejudice	preoccupy	prepare
prerequisite	presumptuous	prevalent
principal	principle	privilege
probably	procedure	proceed
processor	profession	professor
programmed	prominent	prototype
publicly	pursue	purveyor
quantitative	questionnaire	queuing
quiescent	quiet	quit
quite	quorum	quota
rapport	rarefied	receive
recommend	reconcile	reconnoiter
recur	recurrence	reestablish
reexamine	referring	repetition
rhythm	sacrilegious	salable
semiannual	sense	separate
separation	serviceable	shining
similar	sizable	skeptic
stabilize	straitjacket	studying
subcommittee	succeed	succession
supersede	surprise	synonymous
technique	than	their
then	there	they're
thorough	threshold	to
too	trail	trial
transferred	traveler	tremendous
uncorroborated	unduly	unnecessary
unprincipled	validate	vendor
vice versa	viewpoint	villian

wholly	willpower	workday
work flow	work force	workload
worthwhile	wrongdoing	wrongful

USEFUL REFERENCES

The Elements of Style, W. Strunk, Jr., and E. B. White (New York: Macmillan Publishing Co., 1979).

Webster's Ninth New Collegiate Dictionary (Springfield, Mass.: G. & C. Merriam Company, 1987).

The Chicago Manual of Style, 13th edition (Chicago: The University of Chicago Press, 1982).

Words into Type, third edition, (Englewood Cliffs, N.J.: Prentice-Hall, Inc., 1974).

A Dictionary of Modern English Usage, second edition. H. W. Fowler (New York: Oxford University Press, 1965).

Roget's International Thesaurus, fourth edition (New York: Harper & Row, 1977).

Index